Giant killers

ISBN: 978-178456-668-5

Perfect Bound

First published 2019 by UPFRONT PUBLISHING

Peterborough, England.

An environmentally friendly book printed and bound in England

by www.printondemand-worldwide.com

Giant Killers

The History of Posh in the FA Cup.

By

Ray Cole & Dene Butler

Sponsored by

The
Posh Supporters Trust

This book is dedicated to Tommy Robson.

A true Posh Legend, who made more FA Cup appearances for Peterborough United than any other player.

"Keep fighting 'Sir' Tommy"

Contents

Forewords

Peter McNamee (Peterborough United from 1955 to 1965)

When I signed for Posh, it was 1955 and I was in the Army, doing my National Service. A scout came up to the camp where I was based near Gretna Green and said they wanted me to come to Peterborough, I`d never even heard of Peterborough and I went around the camp asking "Where`s Peterborough?". But no one knew, not even the English lads. Then, George Swindin the manager came up and I signed for Posh in the NAAFI. When I did come down, all I knew by then was "it`s the last stop before King`s Cross", which someone had told me. I`m glad I did make the move, it was a good move for me and the people of Peterborough really helped me out. It was completely different to where I came from in Glasgow and I`ve been here ever since. When I played for Posh, I can`t remember us ever being knocked out early in the FA Cup, we always had a good run. We were the

Giant Killers of those days. Before every big cup game, we used to go up to Blackpool, to the Norbreck Hotel on the seafront, which was famous for being used by big clubs for training. They worked us hard, running up and down the beach, but we enjoyed it, it was exciting. Being a non-league club then, we knew we had to be sharper and quicker than normal when we came up against the bigger clubs and we worked really hard, but it was brilliant. Then we became a league club and I remember when we played Aston Villa, we could hear over the speakers that the gates had been locked, as there were over 64,000 people inside Villa Park. I felt I had a good game that night and scored, it was brilliant to play well in front of all those people. I loved playing in front of those big crowds and the atmosphere, especially at home was great, I loved it. The London Road pitch was always good to play on and the fans, especially for those big games really geed us up.

The biggest game for us and the best win, was against Arsenal of course and to score the winning goal was incredible. For the first two hours after beating Arsenal it was heaven, we just thought "We`ve done it!", but I can`t remember much after that, as we all went out for a drink and I didn`t have to buy a drink all night! Then on the Monday we all sat in the dressing room, around the radio, waiting to hear who we had in the next round. We looked at the teams left in and decided who we did and didn`t want. We got Swansea, one of the ones we didn`t want. We drew 0-0 at London Road and I remember Derek Dougan putting a header over the bar, that he really should have scored, but he said "I`ve got it sorted lads, we`ll go down to Swansea and get some extra cash, we can beat them". He was probably the only one who thought we could. When we played Chelsea in the next round, we went down to ten men quite early on as Vic Crowe got injured and our goalkeeper, Willie Duff had a brilliant game, he really kept us in it and helped keep the score down, we lost that game 5-1 in the end.

I played against some big clubs and for me, the FA Cup will never change, everyone wants to win the cup.

Peter Lane (Peterborough United Club Historian.)

Many years ago, I absolutely loved the FA Cup competition. I was so excited to listen to the draw when it was broadcast live on the radio, at about 12:30pm on a Monday. I used to rush home from school to listen to those immortal words from the representative of the Football Association, "The next item on the agenda is the draw for the next round of the FA Cup".

I remember one draw in particular, it was January 1965. I waited with bated breath to hear Posh's number; "Number 13 – Peterborough United will play number 2 – Arsenal" "YES! YES!" Along with my family we were so excited to be playing the mighty Arsenal.

Today I have to say, for me the FA Cup is no longer the greatest competition in the world of football. Why? I feel because the big clubs hardly field many, or any of their star players, therefore fielding an inferior side. To me, this cheats the supporters, especially young children who want to see their favourite players from the Premiership teams perform. Winning the FA Cup means little to some of the Premiership clubs these days, so very soon we shall witness two Championship teams competing in the Final, proving how the once greatest competition in the world is no longer the case. However, the Magic of the Cup up to a point has not quite disappeared altogether because the magic is still there for the small clubs, because they now stand more of a chance of becoming Giant Killers.

Anyway, talking about Giant Killers, I am so privileged to be asked to write this foreword for this wonderful book on Peterborough United when we were renowned, long ago, as the most feared club in the country, as Giant Killers. In those magical days, as a young lad I had the pleasure of catching the bus or train with my family, travelling up and down the country supporting my team called POSH. Away trips included Huddersfield, Fulham, Walsall, Ipswich, and Sheffield Wednesday. Then as a Football League club, travelling to Portsmouth, Aston Villa, Newcastle, QPR, Chesterfield, Swansea, Chelsea, Nottingham Forest and Manchester United. Remember, in those earlier days during the 1950's, perhaps one would say that we only beat teams of the lower divisions, but then the gulf between non-league football and the Third Division was far greater than it is today. Plus of course, those games sometimes attracted attendances of over 20,000 to London Road.

Amongst my FA Cup heroes, I must mention the likes of Dennis Emery, Derek Dougan and Peter McNamee. The greatest FA Cup giant killing act for me had to be when Posh defeated the mighty Arsenal 2-1 at London Road in the 4th Round on the 30th January 1965 with Derek Dougan scoring and then Peter McNamee scoring the winner. Yes, it really was that great for our team called POSH!

Introduction

The magic of the greatest cup competition in the world inspires many minnows of the football world to take on and occasionally beat the biggest and richest clubs in the land. We, as Posh fans, must be realistic enough to know we will probably never win the trophy on the hallowed turf of Wembley, but every year that dream is there as we once again set out on the 'Road To Wembley' and wait with anticipation to find out who we will be drawn against in the next round, until that dream ends for another year and we can once again 'concentrate on the league'.
Peterborough United gained quite a reputation in their Midland League days, as a small club to be feared by any Football League club who were drawn against them in the cup. With Posh gaining Football League status themselves, this reputation continued and their FA Cup exploits meant even the 'big boys' of the top divisions must have dreaded being drawn against the 'Mighty Posh'.
Of course, these things work both ways and Posh have themselves been the 'big boys' dumped out of the cup by non-league opposition. But, more often than not, they have had a decent cup-run, especially for a club of our size. Even in defeat, The Posh have put in some very spirited performances against some of the biggest clubs in country.
The FA Cup is a special competition and can bring a bit of excitement to otherwise uneventful seasons for Posh fans, but those same fans have also had their share of embarrassment, heartbreak and 'what-could-have-beens'.
Our little club have been giant killers and also the victims of a giant killing on several occasions, but at the end of the day, we all keep the faith and dream of the next big cup tie, when we are again David slaying Goliath.
Posh have had a reputation to be proud of in the FA Cup over the years and long may it continue.
In the following chapters we have covered every Posh FA Cup

campaign over the past 85 years of Posh`s existence, taking in the highs and the lows. We have also reproduced shortened versions of the actual match reports, from the local media at the time, of many of the significant ties. Also, at the end of the book you can find all the facts, figures, statistics and records from Posh`s illustrious FA Cup history.

Hopefully you will enjoy reading about the Posh players and teams, going back long before most of us were even born. As Posh fans it is all part of our heritage and those Posh heroes of the past should not be allowed to be forgotten, now or in the years to come, as they are all part of the history of the club that has evolved into the Posh that we know and love today.

1. The 1930s

Peterborough United came into existence in 1934, but didn`t compete in the competition in their inaugural season.
Their first foray into the FA Cup, in the **1935/36** season, was not a great success. In their first ever FA Cup match, on Saturday 5th October 1935, they faced Northamptonshire League side, Rushden Town at London Road, in front of a crowd of 4,254 and were duly knocked out, losing 3-0, in the First Qualifying Round. All three Rushden goals were scored in the first half, with Posh finding their opponents 'out of their league'.

Match Report

v Rushden Town, London Road, 1st Qualifying Round, 5th October 1935.

Posh 0 Rushden Town 3

Sadly, for Posh fans the club's first game in the FA Cup was all over within half an hour, with Rushden 3-0 up after just 27 minutes.
Despite showing some early promise, with Frank Macauley heading a corner against the bar, Posh were totally outclassed and Rushden fully deserved their win. Rushden played some good football, moving quickly, passing accurately and shooting with deadly precision whereas Posh relied on individualism and fancy touches which got them nowhere. In fact, the only players to come out of the game with any credit were Arthur Jefferson, Dave Collins and Jack Kendall. Rushden quickly took command of the game and Posh goalkeeper Kendall had to deal with a number of crosses from Pettit, inside a couple of minutes. In the 16th minute Rushden took the lead, when Eyre beat Jefferson and Pettit's centre found Harrison who scored with a wonderful shot. On 23 minutes Harrison turned provider as he passed the ball to Eyre who left Kendall helpless with a tremendous drive whilst the Posh defence literally stood still. Four minutes later Rushden scored again with Harrison tapping the ball into the net. Posh rallied just before half time and although Rushden's goalkeeper Wallington was kept busy, his goal was not really threatened.
Rushden eased off in the second half, but Posh failed to capitalise. Posh did have one serious effort, a Jefferson free-kick from which Wallington conceded a corner and from Harry Willis' corner, Dave Collins shot against the bar.

Posh: Jack Kendall, Arthur Jefferson, Henry Marsden, Ernie Warren, Len Hargreaves, Harry Willis, Arthur Barraclough, Dave Collins, William Upton, Frank Macauley, Gavin Mitchell.

Attendance: 4,254

The following season, **1936/37**, was much more successful, as they saw off Kettering Town 2-0 away from home in the First Qualifying Round, with Ted Chiverton and Jack Wilson scoring Posh`s first FA Cup goals.

Wolverton Town were beaten 3-0 at home in the next round, they had been drawn away, but the tie was reversed and played at London Road at the request of Wolverton Town, who hoped for a bigger share of gate receipts than they would get if they played the game at their home ground.

Peterborough United were notified on Monday that Wolverton, the South Midlands League club, wished to have the venue of their English cup-tie with Peterborough United to-morrow (Saturday) changed from Wolverton to Peterborough. The sanction of the Football Association has since been obtained and the match will therefore be played at the London Road ground at 3 p.m.

Wolverton will thus be assured of sharing in a "gate" of far greater proportions than they would had the game been staged on their ground. In the previous round, Wolverton defeated Westwood Works in the replay at Wolverton on Wednesday week and the takings only amounted to £3. One man went into the stand!

From Peterborough Advertiser 16th October 1936.

The Third Qualifying Round saw Posh gain revenge over Rushden Town, who had knocked them out the previous season, winning 4-2 at London Road. An away tie in the next round, at Biggleswade Town, saw Posh win 2-1, a result which took them to the heady heights of the First Round Proper in just their second season in the competition. They were drawn away at Dartford, but unfortunately lost 3-0, though it was still a remarkable achievement for a club that had been founded just 2½ years earlier.

Match Report

v Dartford, Watling Street, 1st Round, 28th November 1936.

Dartford 3 Posh 0

The Posh's first FA Cup game in the 'proper' rounds was very disappointing as Dartford ran out 3-0 winners at Watling Street.

Posh's performance was poor and in the end they were lucky to only be beaten 3-0. Jack Kendall was Posh's best player making save after save including a penalty in the closing minutes. The Posh forward-line was very poor with Rutherford, Dartford's goalkeeper, having very little to do, in fact only touching the ball with his hands half a dozen times. With Sam Rowbotham at inside-right, the right-wing lacked spark and the left-wing was disappointing with either Jack Briggs or Syd Sims constantly losing the ball.

Continued...

In a lively opening, Dartford penned The Posh in their own half and a long pass from Harron was controlled by Meads who sent in a hard drive which Kendall saved well. The first goal came on 27 minutes when Gardiner, taking up Harron's pass, beat Kendall with a left-foot shot. Two minutes later Meads scored the second with a snap shot from outside the penalty area, the ball going in under Kendall's outstretched arms. Moseley sent Meads away again but Kendall made a magnificent save and pushed out another shot from Meads who caught the ball on the rebound.
Dartford's third goal came two minutes after the interval when Meads netted from Harron's centre.
With this set back Posh seemed to lose all hope and Kendall was kept busy making saves from Meads, Moseley and Gardiner. In the closing minutes Kendall made two fine saves from Moseley and saved Harron's penalty, awarded when Charlie Bisby fouled Meads.

Posh: Jack Kendall, Charlie Wilson, Charlie Bisby, Len Hargreaves, Ted Chiverton, T. Froggart, Jackie Wilson, Harry Roberts, Sam Rowbotham, Jack Briggs, Syd Sims.

Attendance: 3,486

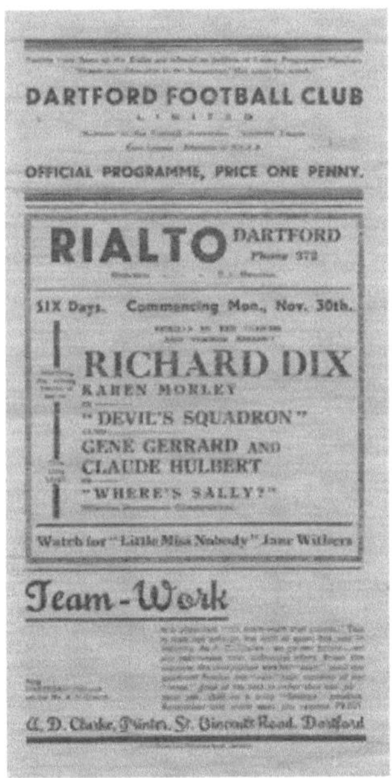

The First Qualifying Round in the **1937/38** season saw Posh put five goals past Wellingborough Town without reply.

Match Report

v Wellingborough Town, The Dog and Duck, 1st Qualifying Round, 2nd October 1937.

Wellingborough Town 0 Posh 5

There was controversy before this game got underway with the pitch being out of shape and the centre line not being centre! Following complaints by the Posh contingent to Mr Noble, the referee, the pitch had to be marked out correctly before a ball was kicked.

Although the Posh ran out comfortable 5-0 winners against their lower league opposition it didn't start well for them, as in the first few minutes Wellingborough broke through the Posh defence time after time and goalkeeper Jack Kendall was called upon to make a save from Orton. Posh did however go ahead on 10 minutes when George Bowater's centre went over the Wellingborough defence with Tommy Atkin following up to head in from close range. The right-winger also notched the second goal, 'rushing' the ball in after his shot had rebounded from the Wellingborough goalkeeper. Wellingborough thought they'd pulled a goal back after Hawtin put the ball past Kendall, but the referee ruled that he had handled and disallowed the goal. Sam Rowbotham scored Posh's third goal after 30 minutes making a clever run from the halfway line and driving the ball with his left foot into the far corner of the net. Posh completed the scoring within fifteen minutes of the re-start with Cyril Boulton scoring both goals. His first came five minutes after the interval, after he beat two backs and fired past Mills in the Wellingborough goal. Ten minutes later after confusion in the Wellingborough defence, Boulton whipped the ball into the net for Posh's fifth goal.

Although they were awarded a couple of penalties Wellingborough were unable to score from them. The first came when Kendall lost the ball with Charles McDonagh catching the ball rugby style on the line. Several Posh players disputed the penalty arguing Kendall had been fouled, but after consulting a linesman the referee gave the penalty which cannoned back off the bar for Clarke to clear. Wellingborough didn't give up hope and when Hawtin was fouled in the area, he took the penalty himself, however this time Kendall saved it.

Posh: Jack Kendall, George Clarke, James Smith, Sam Rowbotham, Harold Smith, Charles McDonagh, Tommy Atkin, Harry Roberts, Cyril Boulton, Reg Foxall, George Bowater.

Attendance: Not Known

The draw for the Second Qualifying Round paired Posh with Kettering Town, who they had beaten the previous season. They came back from 2-0 down at half-time, to draw 2-2 and force a replay at London Road, but Posh bowed out in the replay, losing 1-0 after defender James Smith brought down Kettering`s centre forward Carr, in the penalty area, after just six minutes and Jones scored from the spot. Some good news though, was that the cup run earned Posh £101 1s 10d.

The following season, **1938/39**, saw Posh progress to the First Round Proper again and face a club from the Football League for the first time. In the qualifying rounds they saw off Kettering Town 2-1, then Rushden Town 3-1, thanks to a Charlie McCartney hat-trick, in a replay, following a 4-4 draw in the first match.

Charlie McCartney scored a hat-trick v Rushden Town.

Spalding United, 3-2 were next to go out to Posh and St Neots Town & District were beaten 1-0 in the Fourth Qualifying Round. Posh were drawn against Bristol Rovers of Division 3 (South) in the First Round Proper. The tie at Eastville was only playable as groundsmen worked throughout the night before the game to drain the pitch. Sadly, the pitch was still sodden when the teams took to the field and in front of 7,342 fans the league side beat Posh 4-1, but again the cup run had been a fantastic achievement for a small club like Peterborough United.

Match Report

v Bristol Rovers, Eastville Stadium, 1st Round, 26th November 1938.

Bristol Rovers 4 Posh 1

Although Posh lost, they certainly put up a fight against their Third Division (South) opponents. In fact, the score flattered Rovers as The Posh were never at any stage inferior to the League side and even had three goals disallowed!

Heavy rain throughout the week had waterlogged the Eastville ground and groundsmen worked throughout Friday night with pumps to make the ground playable.

As the game got underway the ground quickly churned up and Posh goalkeeper Dickens soon had plenty to do, however, Posh put together some good moves and Frank White shot just wide and then forced Rovers` keeper Nicholls into a great save from a curling shot. After 20 minutes Rovers went ahead when Curran rammed the ball into the back of the net. The Posh then found the net, but the goal was ruled offside. Dickens was playing a prominent part in The Posh's defence and after half an hour Fielding equalised, the ball came across from the left and he made no mistake with a drive which gave Nicholls no chance. The goal stunned Rovers but Posh could not force home their advantage and five minutes from the interval Curran crossed to Spivey who shot at goal and the ball shot off Warnes' head and then struck McDonagh's shoulder to ricochet into the net.

After the break MacCartney took advantage of a misunderstanding by two Rovers defenders, went clean through but shot wide. Then Haden was left with just Nicholls to beat but his shot was inches away from the target. After 55 minutes Tolland increased Rovers` lead when he shot through a mass of players. Posh continued to attack with MacCartney firing a hard shot at Nicholls before he found the net from a Fielding centre but again the goal was ruled out for offside. Then seven minutes from the end, Tolland put the issue beyond doubt with a fourth goal for Rovers.

Posh: Edward Dickens, Charles McDonagh, Jack Smith, Sam Rowbotham, Frank White, Sam Haden, Horace Fielding, Arthur Sharp, Charlie MacCartney, George Bowater, Fred Warnes.

Attendance: 7,342

The outbreak of the Second World War meant that the FA Cup competition was suspended for the duration of the war.

2. The 1940s

The resumption of the FA Cup came in the **1945/46** season, following the end of hostilities and it was in that season that Posh recorded their biggest ever FA Cup win by beating Rushden Town 9-1 away from home, with Ken Laxton scoring a double hat-trick. Posh went out in the next round though, losing 2-1 away at Kettering Town.

Match Report

Rushden Town v Posh, Hayden Road, 2nd Qualifying Round, 6th October 1945.

Rushden Town 1 Posh 9

The energy and enthusiasm of the Rushden players in the first 10 minutes of this game wore them out completely as Posh went on to register a record win in the FA Cup, beating their local rivals 9-1. Rushden's frantic start to the game rewarded them with a goal on 11 minutes, but straight from the restart Posh equalised through Hubert Tasker and five minutes after that were leading 2-1 through a Rodgers goal. Although it wasn't until the 30th minute that Posh scored their third goal, by this time it was all Posh. The goal scored by Ken Laxton, had the home side appealing for offside, but the referee allowed a goal after consulting his linesman. The fourth goal was scored by Jack Polhill heading in from a Rodgers corner. With two minutes to go to half-time, Rushden goalkeeper Andrews saved a hard drive from Laxton, but could not hold the ball and the centre forward followed up to score.

After five minutes of the second half, Cliff Woods supplied Laxton with an exquisite pass, who shot in from the right of goal. On 65 minutes Laxton scored his fourth and again Woods was the supplier, Laxton controlled his fast pass very neatly before turning the ball past Andrews. The eighth goal came in the 80th minute with Rodgers` close range shot rebounding from the bar to Polhill, who slipped the ball back low to Laxton to score. Laxton's sixth goal was scored in the last minute, the centre forward banging the ball in after a fine piece of work by Polhill.

Posh: William Hilliard, Bernie Bryan, Cyril Parrott, Warner, Tom Hobbs, Jack Polhill, Nobby (Cliff) Woods, Fred Fairchild, Ken Laxton, Hubert Tasker, Rodgers.

Attendance: Not Known

Ken Laxton scored 6 goals against Rushden Town, 6th October 1945.

Season **1946/47** saw Posh progress further in the cup than they had in any previous season. In the qualifying rounds, they beat Wellingborough Town 6-0, with Fred Warnes scoring four times, then Westwood Works (a Baker Perkins works team from the Peterborough League) 3-0, in a tie played at London Road despite Westwood Works being drawn at home. Kettering Town were then beaten 4-1 and Hitchin Town, also 4-1, with Tommy Rudkin scoring a hat-trick. All these ties had been played at London Road, but the First Round Proper saw them play away from home for the first time in that season`s competition, at Yeovil Town. After a 2-2 draw Posh won the replay 1-0, thanks to another Tommy Rudkin goal, his sixth in the FA Cup that season.

Match Report

v Wellingborough Town, London Road, 1st Qualifying Round, 5th October 1946.

Posh 6 Wellingborough Town 0

Despite Wellingborough's brilliant start to this game, within a quarter of an hour they ran out of steam and Posh went on to win with ease.

The result was never in doubt after the 18th minute, when Fred Warnes confused the defence by letting Arnold Bramham's centre go out wide to the right-wing, while Wellingborough`s Kisby and Olney were making up their minds, Alan Scobie nipped in to smash the ball into the roof of the net. Nine minutes later Tommy Rickards slipped a crafty pass to Kisby's right and Warnes followed through on the defender's left to lob the ball over Olney. In the last minute of the half a typical Rickards pass sent Scobie away and a model centre, left Warnes with nothing to do but nod the ball into the net.

Wellingborough were unlucky to lose Rogers, who fell heavily and fractured his arm after a collision with Bryan just after the interval. But that mishap had no bearing on the result. The second half was 26 minutes old before the fourth goal was scored, Kisby made a bad job of covering Bramham's centre and Warnes completed his hat-trick. Warnes scored his fourth ten minutes later, when John Padgett's shot rebounded from a post and found him on the goal line. That had been Padgett's third unlucky effort, the ball beating Olney every time and coming back off the posts. However, he wasn't to be denied a goal as Scobie worked the ball into position for him to net Posh's sixth and final goal of the game.

Posh: Len Silcocks, Bernie Bryan, Cyril Parrott, Tom Smith, Jimmy Smith, Adam Mitchell, Alan Scobie, Tommy Rickards, Fred Warnes, John Padgett, Arnold Bramham.

Attendance: 4,981

Peterborough United 1946/47

Northampton Town of Division 3 (South) were the opponents in the Second Round at London Road, a 1-1 draw meant a replay at the County Ground, which also ended in a 1-1 draw after extra-time, so a second replay, at Coventry City`s Highfield Road, was needed to settle the tie.
This time, The Cobblers were too strong for Posh and ran out 8-1 winners, a result which remains Posh`s heaviest FA Cup defeat.

Match Report

v Northampton Town, Highfield Road, Coventry, 2nd Round 2nd Replay, 23rd December 1946.

Northampton Town 8 Posh 1

Posh's heaviest FA Cup defeat was put down to "the exceptionally heavy strain thrown on the defence by the failure of the attack".
For the first quarter of an hour the Posh defence were their normal selves and there was no reason to suppose that the Posh were about to receive such a drubbing. However, their pace became slower and slower with Cyril Parrott running himself to a standstill and Bernie Bryan severely restricted by an ankle injury. Strange as it may seem, goalkeeper Len Silcocks saved the Posh from a heavier defeat and credit must go to the keeper for a great display. Northampton were in front within two minutes, Garrett placing the ball well wide of Silcocks. This didn't seem to worry Posh as they fought back and 13 minutes later deservedly equalised, Jim Wilson began the move, passing to Alan Scobie, who slipped the ball back to Wilson, as Northampton`s Tom Smalley raced for it, the Posh man punted it to Nat Brooksbank who rounded Northampton keeper John Jones and netted. Posh didn`t stay on level terms for long, as just six minutes later Gordon Roberts ran through unopposed, while the Posh were standing and appealing for offside. After 25 minutes Garrett was allowed to nip in and head home a centre from Alf Morrall. The fourth and fifth goals came from Morrall in the 40th and 55th minutes. Garrett notched the sixth in the 60th minute, Roberts almost walked the ball into the net for the seventh after 73 minutes and with six minutes to go, Garrett scored his fourth goal and Northampton's eighth.

Posh: Len Silcocks, Bernie Bryan, Cyril Parrott, Tommy Rickards, Fred Warnes, Jim Wilson, Alan Scobie, Nat Brooksbank, Arnold Bramham, John Padgett, Tommy Rudkin.

Attendance: 3,164

The following season **1947/48**, Posh knocked out Westwood Works 5-0 at London Road, then Desborough Town 2-1 away and Kettering Town 4-3 away in the first three qualifying rounds, before going out to Vauxhall Motors of Luton 2-1, also away from home, in the Fourth Qualifying Round.

In **1948/49**, Posh made it through the qualifying rounds and into the First Round Proper, where they bowed out to league side Torquay United of Division 3 (South) with a 1-0 defeat at London Road, having beaten Symington`s Recreation (a team from Market Harborough) 4-0 at home, Wellingborough Town 3-2 away, Kettering Town 2-1 at home and Ransome & Marles (a works team from Newark on Trent) 3-1 at home, on their way to the First Round.

The following year **1949/50**, saw a 5-1 win over Desborough Town at home and a 5-0 win away at Kettering Town, before Posh went out 1-0 away at Corby Town in the Third Qualifying Round.

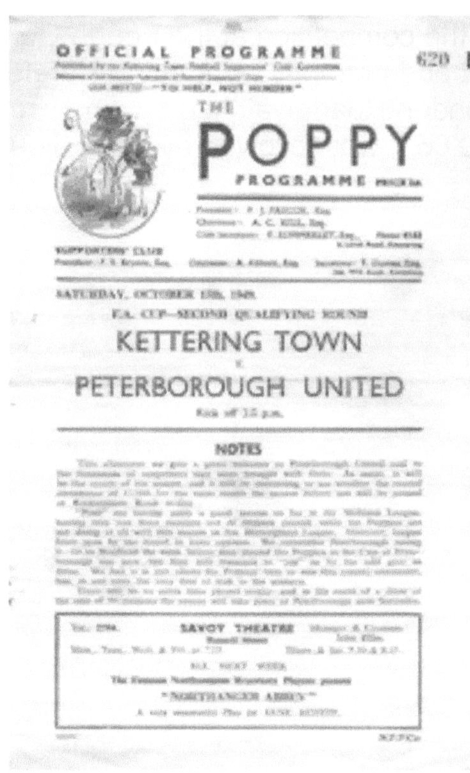

3. The 1950s

This was the decade that Peterborough United, a lowly non-league side from the Midland League really enhanced their reputation as 'giant killers' in the FA Cup, although it was a couple of seasons into the decade before they really got going.

The **1950/51** season saw them beat Symington`s Recreation 3-0, before going out to Kettering Town in the Second Qualifying Round, following a 2-2 draw, they lost the replay 2-1 after extra-time. This was the ninth consecutive FA Cup competition that Posh and Kettering Town had been drawn against each other in the qualifying stages.

Posh came into the competition at the Fourth Qualifying Round stage in **1951/52** and promptly went out to Hereford United, when a 1-1 draw at London Road, watched by a new record attendance of 10,061, was followed by a 1-0 defeat in the replay at Edgar Street.

PETERBOROUGH UNITED FOOTBALL CLUB LIMITED

Hereford United

Official Programme Price 2d.

EMBASSY THEATRE PETERBOROUGH

BOB'S YOUR UNCLE

CHARLES HESLOP

PETER BROUGH and ARCHIE ANDREWS

For sporting people

THE PETERBOROUGH STANDARD

is a winner every week

SPECIALIST COVERAGE OF ALL SPORTS

1952/53 was the season that it all began to happen for Posh and they claimed their first league 'scalp' in the competition. The qualifying rounds saw Posh attracting record crowds wherever they played. They began with a 5-2 win away to Symington`s Recreation, in front of 2,760, a ground record attendance. Then a 3-0 home win over Spalding United in a replay following a 2-2 draw, which also saw a record attendance for The Tulips of 6,228. The next round saw a 5-3 home win over Corby Town after extra time, in a replay following a 0-0 away draw, which once again saw a record attendance of 10,239 for The Steelmen.

Match Report

v Corby Town, London Road, 3rd Qualifying Round Replay, 30th October 1952.

Posh 5 Corby Town 3

Within a minute of the start, Posh were 1-0 up with Freddie Martin scoring with his head from a John Anderson free-kick 40 yards from goal. Straight away Corby fought back, Jack Fairbrother had to get down quickly to stop a close-range shot from Jim Garvey, then twice in quick succession Laird had chances. Corby had another good chance when a cross-field pass found Smith unmarked and although Fairbrother got his body to the ball he failed to hold it, but the winger made a hash of the rebound.

On 18 minutes Posh were 2-0 ahead as Dougald Campbell pulled the ball back from the by-line to George Hair who cracked it home in a flash. United were playing great football and Corby were given little respite. Martin got the ball into the net again, but was given offside. Fairbrother was in action after a long spell of inactivity, punching away Smith's high centre. Then Norman Rigby blocked a strong shot by Fred Slater and Campbell had a chance, but hung on to the ball too long and lost it. There was a moment of anxiety for Fairbrother when the ball glided from Norman Rigby's head and went skimming away towards the corner of the goal, but the keeper made a deft save.

The second half began as sensationally as the first. In the first minute Corby were awarded a penalty, but Jim Garvey missed, shooting high and wide. Corby were now making a fight of it and for a spell had United penned in their own half. In the 68th minute their determination was rewarded when Fairbrother punched away a corner-kick but it fell to the feet of a Corby player who lofted the ball into the air for Salter to head in. Then in the 75th minute came the equaliser, Laird scoring direct from a free-kick on the edge of the penalty-area, shooting the ball over the Peterborough defence. The game developed into a real thriller, with both sides playing desperately for the deciding goal. Three minutes from time Martin was fouled near the by-line and from the penalty-spot Rigby banged the ball into the corner. With less than a minute left, Corby equalised again, Senior put the ball into the goalmouth and in a scramble Garvey ran it into the net.

In the second period of extra time Donaldson challenged the Corby goalkeeper and flashed the ball into the net after Hinton failed to gather cleanly at the foot of a post. Then came the final goal, Campbell running half the length of the field to score in the last minute of the game.

Posh: Jack Fairbrother, Ken Moody, Arnold Woollard, John Anderson, Norman Rigby, Kevin Wood, Dougald Campbell, Paddy Sloan, Andy Donaldson, Freddie Martin, George Hair.

Attendance: 9,845

Then a 2-1 win over Bedford Town at home, saw a new record attendance at London Road of 15,327.

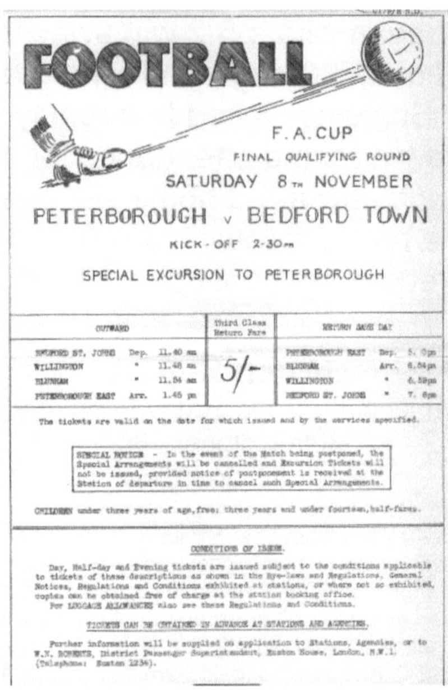

FOOTBALL

F. A. CUP

FINAL QUALIFYING ROUND

SATURDAY 8TH NOVEMBER

PETERBOROUGH v BEDFORD TOWN

KICK-OFF 2-30PM

SPECIAL EXCURSION TO PETERBOROUGH

OUTWARD			Third Class Return Fare	RETURN SAME DAY		
BEDFORD ST. JOHNS	Dep.	11.40 am	5/-	PETERBOROUGH EAST	Dep.	5. 0pm
WILLINGTON	"	11.48 am		BLUNHAM	Arr.	6.54pm
BLUNHAM	"	11.54 am		WILLINGTON	"	6.59pm
PETERBOROUGH EAST	Arr.	1.45 pm		BEDFORD ST. JOHNS	"	7. 6pm

The tickets are valid on the date for which issued and by the services specified.

SPECIAL NOTICE - In the event of the Match being postponed, the Special Arrangements will be cancelled and Excursion Tickets will not be issued, provided notice of postponement is received at the Station of departure in time to cancel such Special Arrangements.

CHILDREN under three years of age, free; three years and under fourteen, half-fares.

CONDITIONS OF ISSUE.

Day, Half-day and Evening tickets are issued subject to the conditions applicable to tickets of these descriptions as shown in the Bye-laws and Regulations, General Notices, Regulations and Conditions exhibited at stations, or where not so exhibited, copies can be obtained free of charge at the station booking office.

For LUGGAGE ALLOWANCES also see these Regulations and Conditions.

TICKETS CAN BE OBTAINED IN ADVANCE AT STATIONS AND AGENCIES.

Further information will be supplied on application to Stations, Agencies, or to W.N. ROBERTS, District Passenger Superintendent, Euston House, London, N.W.1. (Telephone: Euston 1234).

Then in the First Round Proper came the landmark 2-1 win at London Road against Torquay United of Division 3 (South), with Paddy Sloan and Freddie Martin the goal scorers for Posh.

Match Report

v Torquay Utd, London Road, 1st Round, 22nd November 1952.

Posh 2 Torquay United 1

The first half of this cup-tie was goalless and at times United's play was scrappy, unlike their second half performance.

Freddie Martin scored United's first goal on 60 minutes, nipping between full-back Drinkwater and the advancing Torquay goalkeeper to hook the ball home. Just 40 seconds later Donaldson had the ball in the net again, calmly finishing from Freddie Martin's pass across the goal-line. Initially referee Mr Clapton appeared to signal a goal, however after consulting one of his linesmen he gave Torquay a free-kick, indicating Donaldson was offside. At this stage United had the Torquay defence in a tangle and might well have built up a big score had the goal stood. However, the let-off gave Torquay heart and they were soon hammering the United defence. It was here that Fairbrother reigned supreme as he made a succession

Continued...

of first-class saves. Sadly, the Posh goal was finally breached with Fairbrother scooping the ball up in a scrummage on the goal-line, but the referee blew for a goal. No one seemed to know who applied the finishing touch with either Collins or Edds getting the final touch. With only 10 minutes left to play United looked set for a replay, until Donaldson set Martin off down the left-wing, where he centred for Paddy Sloan to head the ball into the net.
A great win for Peterborough with every team member playing a valuable part.

Posh: Jack Fairbrother, Ken Moody, Arnold Woollard, John Anderson, Norman Rigby, Kevin Wood, Dougald Campbell, Paddy Sloan, Andy Donaldson, Freddie Martin, George Hair.

Attendance:12,938

The glorious run came to an end in the Second Round against Bristol Rovers, again at London Road and this time in front of another crowd of over 15,000 fans, with Rovers winning 1-0.

Peterborough United 1952/53

The following year **1953/54**, Posh were at it again. They beat Grays Athletic 4-1 in the Fourth Qualifying Round and Hitchin Town 3-1 in the First Round Proper, before Aldershot became the second league club to suffer at the hands of Peterborough United following a 2-1 win for Posh at London Road, with the attendance record once again broken, as 16,743 fans saw Freddie Martin and Doug Taft score the Posh goals. After the game, manager Jack Fairbrother announced he was leaving the club to manage Coventry City, but he would not move on while Posh were still in the cup. The win meant Posh progressed to the Third Round for the first time and the possibility of being drawn against one of the big boys from the top two divisions and they weren`t disappointed, as they were drawn against Cardiff City of the First Division. In what was Jack Fairbrother`s last game in charge of Posh (at least for the time-being), in front of 38,000 at Ninian Park, Posh took a shock early lead through Freddie Martin, but despite putting up a brave fight, they eventually went down 3-1.

Match Report

v Cardiff City, Ninian Park, 3rd Round, 9th January 1954.

Cardiff City 3 Posh 1

United kicked off the game in their brand new red shirts and were already playing some good football before taking the lead on 5 minutes, Barry Matthews cut the ball back to George Hair whose shot beat Ron Howells in the Cardiff goal, with Freddie Martin by the foot of the post to net. Cardiff responded swiftly putting on the pressure with some clever passing and Trevor Ford equalised from close range in the 14th minute after a neat pass from George Edwards. The Posh defence were under a lot of pressure, with Fairbrother punching out a Tommy Northcott shot after superb approach play by the home side had split the United defence, then just before half time, Ford missed an open-goal after a bad back-pass.

Posh started strongly in the second-half but Cardiff still threatened the United goal with Fairbrother twice saving well from Ford and Dougald Campbell clearing a dangerous situation by sprinting away from the goal-line to the halfway line. Fairbrother continued to make a number of saves but United kept plugging away and created a number of chances. Then just 10 minutes from the end, Ford scored with a hard, high cross and with United tiring Cardiff became more dangerous. With 4 minutes to go Nortcott ran through the middle and from point-blank range Fairbrother saved but the ball fell right for the inside-forward and he only had to tap the ball into the net. Still United went on the attack and Hair squared the ball, but Howells just beat Campbell and Matthews to the ball.

Although United had a lot of luck they played good football throughout and deserved praise for their gallant efforts.

Posh: Jack Fairbrother, Ken Moody, George Hall, John Anderson, Norman Rigby, Paddy Sloan, Dougald Campbell, Freddie Martin, Doug Taft, Barry Matthews, George Hair.

Attendance: 38,000

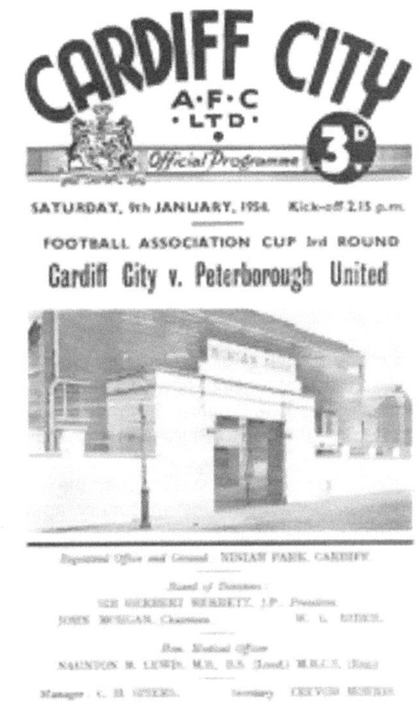

By comparison, **1954/55** was a complete flop, with Posh exiting to Boston United at the first hurdle, in the Fourth Qualifying Round, with a 2-1 home defeat, the only thing of note about the game was that the Posh goal was scored by Dennis Emery, who then went on to score in Posh`s next nine consecutive FA Cup ties.

But **1955/56** saw Posh add to their reputation. After a 3-1 win over Ilkeston Town in the Fourth Qualifying Round, they faced Ipswich Town, a Division 3 (South) side at the time, who were managed Alf Ramsey, in the First Round Proper and earned themselves a memorable 3-1 win, in front of another new record attendance at London Road of 20,671.

Match Report

v Ipswich Town, London Road, 1st Round, 19th November 1955.

Posh 3 Ipswich Town 1

This was not only a great result but a great day with every United player playing well and giving their all.

The game began evenly and for 20 minutes it was anyone's game with United just having the edge. Andy Donaldson got in the first real shot of the game, after about 20 minutes and seven minutes later he had a hand in United's first goal, he pushed a pass from Bernard Shaw to Bob Gibson who sent the ball across for Dennis Emery to score. The cheers had hardly subsided when George Hair had the ball in the net again, it looked as though he outran a defender to a high cross and crashed it home with his head. But the referee ruled the goal offside. Peterborough had a few narrow escapes, in particular when Wilf Grant hit the upright and Jerry Lowery made a number of good saves. Playing a closer passing game, Ipswich looked dangerous when they got moving, particularly their right-winger Billy Reed who gave Roy Killin a hard time. It was Reed that made the Ipswich equaliser, as he beat Killin and centred, Blackman headed the ball towards goal with Tommy Parker putting it into the net.

In the second half Peterborough dominated and straight from the kick-off they went for goal. United's second goal came 12 minutes after the restart, Emery, again working hard, sent the ball into the goalmouth, Donaldson, Gibson and goalkeeper McMillan went for it, but the ball curved over their heads into the net. With the crowd roaring for more, just 5 minutes later Peterborough were 3-1 ahead with the best goal of the game. George Hair outran the defence with the ball at his feet and shot, McMillan parried the ball, Hair still running in met it with his head and it was in the back of the net. Ipswich fought back with half-back John Elsworthy doing two men's work, but they could not break the Peterborough defence and rarely did they get past Rigby and if they did Lowery was on form.

Posh: Jerry Lowery, Jim Clarke, Roy Killin, Bernard Shaw, Norman Rigby, Des Farrow, Billy Hails, Dennis Emery, Andy Donaldson, Bob Gibson, George Hair.

Attendance: 20,671

The Second Round paired Posh with Swindon Town, also a Division 3 (South) side and after a 1-1 draw away, they went out 2-1 after extra-time, in the replay at London Road.

The **1956/57** season`s cup run for Posh began with a 5-1 win against Corby Town in the Fourth Qualifying Round, then a 3-1 win, in the First Round Proper, over Yeovil Town. In the Second Round, Posh showed their ability to beat league opposition was no fluke, by knocking out Bradford Park Avenue of Division 3 (North) with a 3-0 victory. The Third Round paired Posh with Second Division side Lincoln City, a 2-2 draw at London Road attracted another new record attendance of 22,000 and was followed by a replay at Sincil Bank. In a dramatic match, Posh won 5-4 after extra-time, with Andy Donaldson scoring a hat-trick, although it was reported in the local press that he was taken ill before the game and was given a brandy and port pick-me-up by the trainer!

Match Report

v Lincoln City, Sincil Bank, 3rd Round Replay, 9th January 1957.

Lincoln City 4 Posh 5 (after extra-time)

What a cracking cup tie this turned out to be.

In the first 2 minutes Peterborough had two good chances to score and after just 8 minutes they went ahead, Jack Hogg pushed the ball to Ray Barr who swung the ball into the middle where Ray Smith shot, the Lincoln keeper got to the ball but could not hold it and Andy Donaldson ran in to score. Lincoln were soon on the attack with Bannan just missing, before appealing strongly for a penalty, for handball against Bernard Shaw, the referee waved play on and as the ball ran loose, Neal drove the ball goal-bound but Jack Walls somehow tipped the ball over the crossbar. Then after 19 minutes Lincoln equalised, Bannan flicking the ball past Walls from Watson's pass. However, after 22 minutes Peterborough were ahead again when Donaldson hooked the ball past Downie from a pass from the right. Danger continued to threaten the Peterborough goal but they were in no way inferior to Lincoln who seemed to lack Peterborough's will to fight for every ball.

In the second half Lincoln played much better and play was end to end. Emery scored but the referee ruled the goal out for offside, then Northcott hit the United post with Walls well beaten. With just 2 minutes left, Lincoln equalised, a free-kick by Munro was headed home by Neal and so the game went into extra time.

Peterborough made nearly all the running in the opening minutes of extra-time and after 14 minutes, a pass by Hails sent Donaldson away on the right-wing, he beat Troops, ran in and put over a cross which Emery scored from.

In the 4th minute of the second period of extra-time, Smith cracked home a pass from Shaw to make it 4-2 and three minutes later, from Hogg's centre, Donaldson headed the best goal of the match. Northcott scored Lincoln's third two minutes from time and Bannan scored for Lincoln from the penalty spot a minute later.

Posh: Jack Walls, Norman Douglass, Ray Barr, Bernard Shaw, Norman Rigby, Henry Cockburn, Billy Hails, Dennis Emery, Ray Smith, Andy Donaldson, Jack Hogg.

Attendance: 18,216

So Posh entered the previously uncharted territory of the FA Cup Fourth Round, where they faced Second Division side Huddersfield Town who had 16-year-old Dennis Law in their team. Approximately 10,000 Posh fans made up the crowd of 48,735, but the dream ended in a spirited 3-1 defeat and it was the game in which Dennis Emery`s run of scoring in ten consecutive FA Cup matches came to an end.

Match Report

v Huddersfield Town, Leeds Road, 4th Round, 26th January 1957.

Huddersfield Town 3 Posh 1

Playing against a club that only one season ago were in the First Division, United did nothing but enhance their reputation despite losing the match 3-1.

For the vast majority of the game Posh held Huddersfield to a one-goal lead, they even got within striking distance of a replay.

Despite Denis Law scoring after just 2 minutes, Posh showed plenty of skill, in particular Dennis Emery and Billy Hails, with Henry Cockburn showing what a great footballer he still is. However, against opposition like this Peterborough's weaknesses were exposed. Too much close play and the reluctance to shoot were tactical mistakes that were to cost United dearly. Town's defence seemed impenetrable, but despite this Emery had two chances in the early stages of the game but sadly he did not take advantage of them. Still in the first half, United should have been awarded a penalty for a trip on Hails but referee Mr Cooper dismissed Peterborough's appeal.

As for the second half, where for long periods, particularly up to Town's second goal, United were in great form, playing good football and keeping the opposition in their own half. However, in the 66th minute Jack Walls made his only error of the game to give Dave Hickton an easy goal. The goal had a dampening effect on United, but Shaw's deserved penalty in the 83rd minute put new life back into the Posh and the next 5 minutes were as exciting as anyone could wish for. Then another quick break by Law and Ron Simpson made it 3-1 to Town, with just a minute to go.

Posh: Jack Walls, Norman Douglass, Ray Barr, Bernard Shaw, Norman Rigby, Henry Cockburn, Billy Hails, Dennis Emery, Ray Smith, Andy Donaldson, Jack Hogg.

Attendance: 48,735

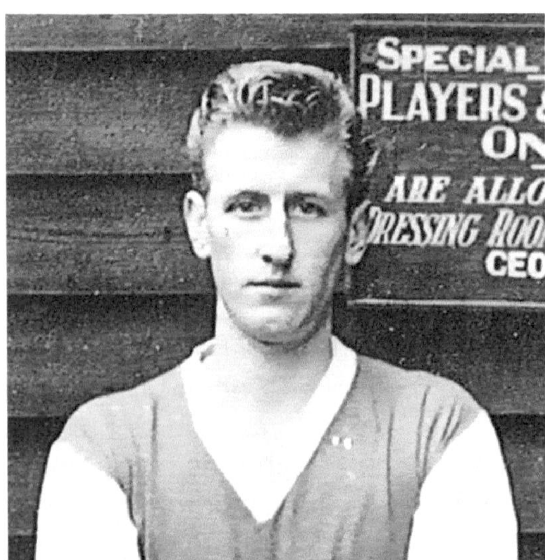

Dennis Emery scored in every Posh FA Cup match from 6th November 1954 to 9th January 1957.

The following season, **1957/58** Posh progressed to the First Round Proper by beating Wolverton Town & BR 7-0 in the Fourth Qualifying Round with Jimmy Longworth netting a hat-trick, but then then lost away to Torquay United 1-0 in a replay, following a 3-3 draw at home.

In **1958/59** Posh beat Walthamstow Avenue 3-0 at home, with Dennis Emery scoring all three goals, in the Fourth Qualifying Round.

Action from Posh v Walthamstow Avenue Fourth Qualifying Round 1st November 1958

They then beat Kettering Town 3-2 after extra-time in a First Round replay at Rockingham Road, after drawing 2-2 at London Road. In the Second Round they beat Headington United (now known as Oxford United) 4-2. The Third Round saw them take Second Division Fulham, with England internationals George Cohen, Jimmy Hill and Johnny Haynes in their side, to a replay. The Cottagers narrowly won the replay 1-0 at London Road, after Posh had held them to a goalless draw, at Craven Cottage.

Match Report

v Fulham, Craven Cottage, 3rd Round, 10th January 1959.

Fulham 0 Posh 0

United not only tamed Second Division Fulham, but almost knocked them out of the cup. With a little bit of luck Peterborough would have been through to the Fourth Round already, instead of facing a replay at London Road.

Had both Dennis Emery and Billy Hails had a little bit of luck with their efforts they would have got at least one past the magnificent Tony Macedo in the Fulham goal. Hails flying header, minutes after the restart, was so unlucky not to go in.

However, there was one piece of luck on Peterborough's side, when Johnny Haynes went down in the penalty area and the referee bizarrely awarded a goal-kick instead of a penalty-kick. Fulham would have been out of the cup had it not been for goalkeeper Macedo and Jim Langley's sterling efforts to infuse some sort of punch into Fulham. Apart from goals, Peterborough were the better team, in charge of the play and much more confident than their opponents. Other than Leggat, none of the Fulham forward-line tried their luck with a shot. Peculiar when they had Haynes who made several useful openings for the forwards. The Peterborough defence didn't look certain early on in the game, but Fulham didn't take advantage of that.

Jimmy Hill was only a pale shadow of his old self and Dennis Emery outshone him. It was one of those days when Emery showed everyone what a great player he is and what 'bigger clubs' have missed. But perhaps it's unfair to single out individuals in this gallant side. The forwards always moved with more purpose than Fulham's. The defence shook off its early uncertainty and in goal, Jack Walls was equal to everything.

The Posh: Jack Walls, Ellis Stafford, Jim Walker, Derek Chadwick, Roy Banham, Norman Rigby, Billy Hails, Dennis Emery, Ray Smith, Jim Rayner, Peter McNamee.

Attendance: 31,908

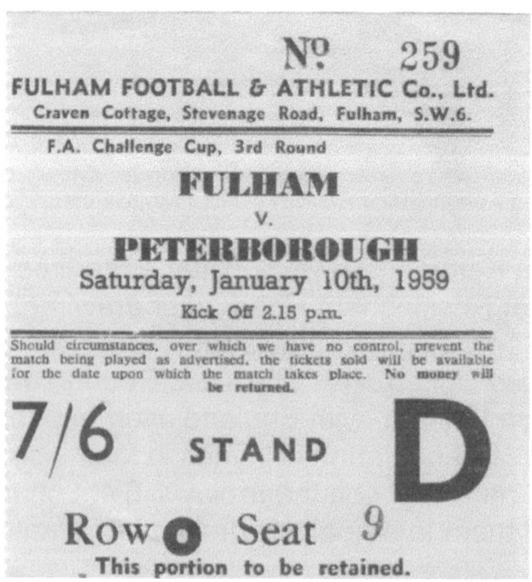
Nº 259
FULHAM FOOTBALL & ATHLETIC Co., Ltd.
Craven Cottage, Stevenage Road, Fulham, S.W.6.
F.A. Challenge Cup, 3rd Round
FULHAM
v.
PETERBOROUGH
Saturday, January 10th, 1959
Kick Off 2.15 p.m.
Should circumstances, over which we have no control, prevent the match being played as advertised, the tickets sold will be available for the date upon which the match takes place. No money will be returned.
7/6 STAND D
Row O Seat 9
This portion to be retained.

Match Report

v Fulham, London Road, 3rd Round Replay, 24th January 1959.

Posh 0 Fulham 1

This game was full of drama straight from the kick-off, as Posh went into the attack. They forced the first corner of the game after only 30 seconds and it was only a solo effort by Jimmy Hill which reduced pressure on the visitors' defence. However, United were soon back on the attack with Dennis Emery just failing to control the ball when in a good shooting position. The first real shock to United's defence came after seven minutes when Johnny Haynes slid a great pass through to Hill in front of goal, Hill let fly with a strong shot, but miraculously Posh's goalkeeper Jack Walls managed to palm the ball away for a corner.

Two shots from left-winger Peter McNamee were deflected for corners and then when Billy Hails tricked Jim Langley, Fulham goalkeeper Tony Macedo grabbed the ball desperately on the goal-line to prevent a goal. Langley injured himself attempting to stop Hails and he left the field for treatment, returned to play for a few minutes on the right-wing and then finally went off for good. Fulham rearranged their team as United piled on the pressure, but several minutes before Langley's final departure from the field Fulham scored. It was a chaotic affair, Leggat's corner-kick found Hill, who shot hurriedly for goal, his shot was sliced to Johnson who deflected it past Walls before he could react. United hit back and had Fulham reeling with shots from Emery and Chadwick going close. Then Fulham were unlucky when Walls was beaten by a free-kick and Norman Rigby headed off the goal-line. Then came the miss of the match, Hails cut in from the wing and sent in a good, low shot, the ball beat Macedo, rebounded into the goalmouth, Jim Rayner rushed in to put the ball into the empty goal but scooped it over the crossbar.

Posh completely dominated the game in the second half and did everything but score. Rayner went out on the right-wing and Hails was moved into the centre but the move did not pay off. What few shots there were, were easily held by Macedo or rebounded to safety off a wall of defenders. Banham almost equalised with a great rising shot from outside the penalty area and although the ball beat Macedo, it struck the underside of the crossbar and was scrambled clear. Until the dying seconds, United tried desperately to rally, one goal would have meant survival, but sadly it never came.

Posh: Jack Walls, Ellis Stafford, Jim Walker, Derek Chadwick, Roy Banham, Norman Rigby, Billy Hails, Dennis Emery, Ray Smith, Jim Rayner, Peter McNamee.

Attendance: 21,600

In the **1959/60** season, Posh`s last as a non-league club, they knocked no less than three league clubs out of the competition. A 7-1 win in the Fourth Qualifying Round at London Road, against Bury Town was followed by a First Round home win over Shrewsbury Town 4-3, a Second Round victory away at Walsall 3-2 and a Third Round win over Second Division Ipswich Town, 3-2 at Portman Road.

Match Report

v Ipswich Town, Portman Road, 3rd Round, 9th January 1960.
Ipswich Town 2 Posh 3

At times playing in a blizzard, Peterborough pulled off yet another great cup win.
The home side seemed to have cup match nerves, with pass after pass going astray in the early stages of the game and Peterborough, without doubt on top at this stage, had a number of good efforts on the Ipswich goal. However, eventually Ipswich came more into the game, playing really clever football now and after Roy Banham had slipped, Daley saved a point-blank shot from Crawford. On 19 minutes, following a disputed corner, Ipswich took the lead. Crawford went up with Daley and his header was cleared off the line by Walker, but Millward was following up and cracked the ball into the net. Ipswich kept up terrific pressure and it was Peterborough who were now sending passes astray. The home side were mastering the conditions well and in quick succession, both Leadbetter and Crawford missed golden opportunities. When the snow stopped, Peterborough looked more sure of themselves and started to look dangerous. Then on 42 minutes Posh equalised, when McNamee pushed the ball to Smith, whose low cross was slammed to the back of the net by Rayner. Just before half time Jim Walker was injured and left the field, although he returned after the interval, his injury restricted his game significantly.
Within a minute of the restart Ipswich were back in the lead, from a movement on the left, Phillips shot towards goal, the ball hit the upright and as it came back the same player shot again to give Ipswich their second goal. After a Posh re-shuffle, McNamee surged his way past two men to give Emery the ball, and he calmly slipped the ball into the net in the 51st minute. The Ipswich forwards were still a great menace and the goalmouth scramble from a cross from Millward was only ended when the referee gave a handball decision in Peterborough's favour. With three minutes left of play Peterborough took the lead, from a Banham throw-in the ball went to McNamee and a mis-kick by a defender let in Emery who scored Posh's third goal of the game. Ipswich re-started the game in a blizzard and even though they had nothing to lose and put everything into the game Posh continued to attack and held out for another famous cup win.

Posh: Tom Daley, Ellis Stafford, Jim Walker, Roy Banham, Norman Rigby, Derek Chadwick, Billy Hails, Denis Emery, Jim Rayner, Ray Smith, Peter McNamee.

Attendance: 26,000

The Fourth Round draw paired Posh with First Division Sheffield Wednesday at Hillsborough, where approximately 15,000 Posh supporters made up a crowd of 51,144. Posh held out until just twelve minutes from the end, but two quick goals gave Wednesday a 2-0 win.

Match Report

v Sheffield Wednesday, Hillsborough, 4th Round, 30th January 1960.

Sheffield Wednesday 2 Posh 0

Straight from the kick-off the Peterborough defence was under the cosh, with Wednesday playing delightful football and their forwards` speed causing the United defence real problems.

With 10 minutes gone, Peterborough had not had a shot at goal and had received their first taste of First Division tackling, finding the Sheffield defence as fast as their forwards. Daley was brought to his knees by a Fantham shot and the goalkeeper's long kick sent Hails away, but Peterborough's forward line were finding Peter Swan a rock in the Sheffield defence. Peterborough kept pegging away, but after 25 minutes of play they had still made little impression on the Sheffield defence. Banham made a desperate tackle to prevent Kay from getting in a shot and the ball was put away for a corner, Finney took the kick, but Rigby cleared. Centre-forward Griffin tried to round Rigby but ended up with his face in the snow. Tony Kay, who was proving a scourge to the visitors, made a 40-yard run down the field only to fluff his shot when 10 yards out from goal. Fast, though Peterborough were, Sheffield were even faster and produced the kind of fine football which had earned them fourth place in the First Division. It was Craig who initiated another Sheffield attack, but Ellis Stafford brilliantly intercepted his pass out to Finney. Ray Smith sent Hails away and the winger collided with Springett, who had come out of his goal, near the edge of the box, but the England goalkeeper was soon on his feet with the help of the sponge. Peterborough had a remarkable escape when Griffin took the ball close in to goal and hooked it back only to find Wilkinson a little too much ahead to do anything. Peterborough went on the attack, but the cheers turned to boos when Hails collapsed near the penalty spot, apparently elbowed in the face by goalkeeper Springett, the referee allowed play to go on and bounced the ball in the centre-circle after Hails had recovered! A few seconds before half time Peterborough earned their first corner, but the whistle blew before anything could come of it.

Emery and McNamee started the second half with a delightful move down the left-wing, but it ended as suddenly as it began when the inside-forward's pass went astray. Peterborough looked far more dangerous with McNamee seeing more of the ball, but even he found Wednesday a problem. Emery started the fans roaring with one of his typical cross-field moves, which ended with Hails being brought down in the area but the referee waved play on. Peterborough found themselves hemmed in, in their own half, as the Sheffield side looked to get the important goal to break the deadlock. With 20 minutes left to play it was still anyone's match and it looked as though Peterborough could at least hang on for a replay. After some fine work by McAnearney, Craig sent a shiver down Peterborough's spine with a 30-yard rocket which passed close by the post and it was the same player, Craig, who put Sheffield in front with 12 minutes to go, with a brilliant shot from 30 yards which went in via the top of the post. Seconds later Wilkinson had a chance to increase the lead, but he was far too slow. Three minutes later it was Craig again who rammed in number two from close in, after Finney had whipped past two Peterborough defenders.

Posh: Tom Daley, Ellis Stafford, Jim Walker, Roy Banham, Norman Rigby, Derek Chadwick, Billy Hails, Dennis Emery, Jim Rayner, Ray Smith, Peter McNamee.

Attendance: 51,144

Posh fan Dusty Hall prepares for the match against Sheffield Wednesday at Hillsborough.

Posh had certainly by this time gained a reputation as FA Cup 'Giant Killers' with no less than seven different league 'scalps' under their belt and were awarded the 'Sunday Pictorial Giant Killers Cup'.

4. The 1960s

With Posh now a Football League club themselves, they no longer had to play in the qualifying rounds, although they had for several years been entering the competition at the Fourth Qualifying Round stage.

Posh went on a winning tour of the South Coast in the first three rounds of the cup in **1960/61**, beating Dover 4-1 away in the First Round, Third Division Torquay United 3-1 away in the Second Round and then Posh were once again 'Giant Killers' as they beat Second Division Portsmouth 2-1 in the Third Round at Fratton Park, with Keith Ripley and Billy Hails scoring the Posh goals.

Match Report

v Portsmouth, Fratton Park, 3rd Round, 7th January 1961.

Portsmouth 1 Posh 2

Posh had to beat both Portsmouth and the mud to get through this game and reach the 4th Round of the cup.

The Posh defence played magnificently and rarely put a foot wrong. At times it seemed as though Pompey must score, but there was always a Posh defender on hand and the home team finally resorted to long-range shots. Both wing-halves, Jim Rayner and Keith Ripley struggled to break up attacks in midfield, but they successfully stuck to their task in the muddy conditions. Both teams had seen shots rebound from the woodwork before a Ripley snap-shot just before half time, after a right-wing attack that had only been partly cleared, broke the deadlock. It wasn't until half time that the majority of spectators found out that the referee had allowed the goal!

Early on in the second half Posh almost scored again, but then Portsmouth, who dominated the game, forced United back in defence and they deserved their equaliser on 77 minutes when left-winger Wilson headed home. However, Pompey tired and United got a second-wind as they played out the remaining minutes of the game full of confidence and determination. With the referee looking at his watch the ball went across the entire United attack, Ray Smith had a chance to shoot but he slipped the ball to Billy Hails and with only former international Jimmy Dickinson between him and a shot at goal, Hails nipped past Dickinson and shot from an acute angle. The ball hit the back of the net before the Portsmouth goalkeeper had begun his dive to give United a 2-1 lead. There was just time to restart the game before jubilant Posh fans took over at Fratton Park to celebrate yet another fantastic FA Cup upset.

Posh: Jack Walls, Dick Whittaker, Jim Walker, Jim Rayner, Norman Rigby, Keith Ripley, Billy Hails, Dennis Emery, Terry Bly, Ray Smith, Peter McNamee.

Attendance: 27,533

Captain Norman Rigby (right) before Posh`s win over Portsmouth 7th January 1961

They were drawn at home to Aston Villa of the First Division in the Fourth Round and held them to a 1-1 draw, thanks to a Billy Hails goal, earning a replay at Villa Park. Four days later, the crowd of 64,531 at Villa Park was the biggest crowd any Posh team had, or has since, played in front of, but many more fans were locked out of the ground. They saw Posh bow out in a narrow 2-1 defeat, with Peter McNamee on the scoresheet for Posh. The Villa team included Welsh international and future Posh player, Vic Crowe.

Match Report

v Aston Villa, London Road, 4th Round, 28th January 1961.

Posh 1 Aston Villa 1

This game will perhaps be remembered for the atrocious weather conditions in which it was played, as torrential rain made the pitch a quagmire, but despite this, both sides gave hearty displays.

Both Villa players and supporters got the shock of their lives by the skill, enthusiasm and stamina shown by Posh. Posh presented a very solid rearguard with Jim Walker and Dick Whittaker in command of nearly every situation. Wing-halves Jim Rayner and Keith Ripley were courageous in tackles and blotted out the Villa inside-forwards for long periods. It was Billy Hails who got United's only goal after 30 minutes but most of the credit must go to Peter McNamee, for it was McNamee who controlled a long curving pass from Dennis Emery before twisting past Villa full-back Neal, then beat another inrushing defender before crossing the ball to Hails, who took ages before side-stepping several paces towards the centre of the goal, then flicking the ball home.

Roy Banham had the difficult task of keeping centre-forward Gerry Hitchens under control, but he did it well. It was therefore, unfortunate that Roy scored Villa's goal which gave them a replay. Jack Walls came out to block a Hitchens shot and the quick-thinking centre-forward poked out a foot in a bid to flick the ball across to his right-winger, but the ball struck Walls on the leg, bounced up into Banham's face and the ball was deflected into the goal. Banham tried desperately to reach the ball, but he could only watch in horror as it rolled over the line. Jack Walls was hurt in the incident, but after treatment continued and produced a great performance. He was twice beaten by Hitchens and McParland, but both goals were disallowed by the referee. Jack's best save came when O'Neill drew him out of goal and chipped the ball over his head, but somehow Jack managed to get his fingertips to the ball. It was a shame Posh couldn't turn their second-half supremacy into goals, as in the last few minutes of the game Villa were a beaten team.

Posh: Jack Walls, Dick Whittaker, Jim Walker, Jim Rayner, Roy Banham, Keith Ripley, Billy Hails, Dennis Emery, Terry Bly, Ray Smith, Peter McNamee.

Attendance: 28,266

Vic Crowe played against Posh for Aston Villa.

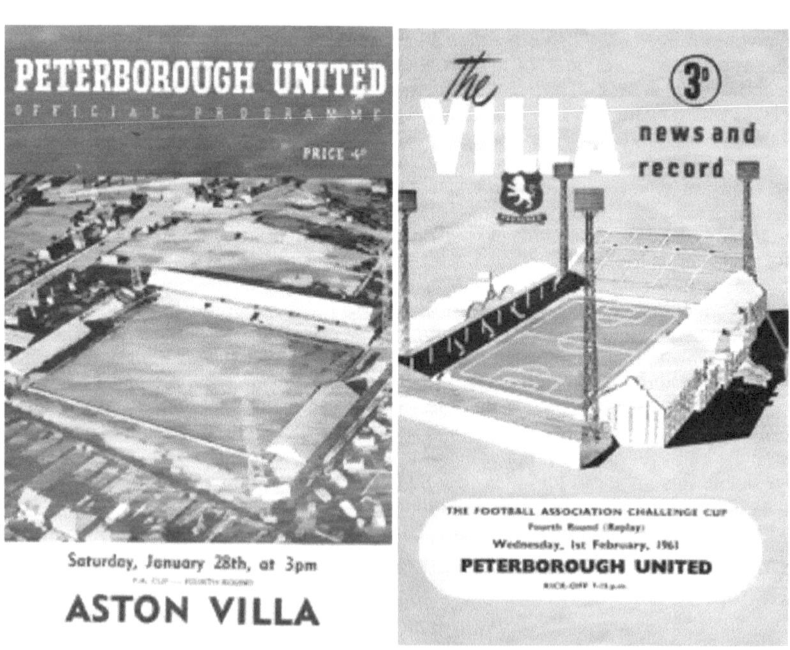

Match Report

v Aston Villa, Villa Park, 4rd Round Replay, 1st February 1961.

Aston Villa 2 Posh 1

Two goals from Aston Villa's Irish international Peter McParland ended Posh's hopes of a 5th Round FA Cup match with Tottenham Hotspur at London Road.

Villa made all the running in the opening minutes of the game and very nearly took the lead in their first attack, when Hitchens saw his shot go inches wide of the post with Walls groping for the ball. A shot from Emery was deflected for United's first corner and it soon became apparent that the home side were not going to have things all their own way. Then it was McParland's turn to give Posh a scare, as he was presented with a great opportunity by Hitchens and as he cut in from the wing he unleashed a tremendous shot which Walls blocked with his body but could not hold, the ball was scrambled away, but the power of McParland's shot winded the United keeper and he had to receive attention from Johnnie Anderson. Walls was soon in the thick of it again when MacEwan ran in with only the Posh goalkeeper to beat, miraculously Walls got his body in the way of the ball again and the danger was cleared. Then came another brilliant diving save from Walls, to put a tremendous shot on the run from MacEwan round the post. Terry Bly was unlucky when he leapt to meet a centre from McNamee and beat goalkeeper Potter in the air, only to see the ball hit a defender and bounce to safety. Slowly and surely Posh began to take the upper hand and Villa had to resort to deceitful tactics, McParland diving twice in succession in the penalty area in a bid to get a penalty.

Within four minutes of the restart Villa snatched the lead, there appeared little danger as O'Neill ran down the right with the ball, but his centre deceived the Posh defence and Walls was left stranded as McParland brought the ball under control and blasted it into the corner of the net. But, United were far from disheartened, they increased the pressure on Villa goalkeeper Potter and nearly scored, when a free-kick from Ripley was only inches outside an upright. Potter was again left groping for the ball in the air from a McNamee corner-kick and although Emery tried to tee the ball up by heading it down to Bly, the centre-forward's shot was deflected for another corner-kick. Villa began to lose their poise and Ripley took advantage of several free-kicks to give Potter more worry. On one occasion, Bly and Smith bustled the young goalkeeper over the line with the ball, but the referee awarded a free-kick to Villa. Then, every member of the forward-line came into action before the ball went out to Hails for the final shot, unfortunately his shot rebounded from Potter, hit the onrushing Dugdale and went out for a corner. From the corner-kick however, the ball came out to McNamee who promptly punted it over the heads of the Villa defence into the back of the net via the underside of the crossbar. But, within a minute Villa scored again, the ball bobbled about in the Posh penalty area and McParland seemed to be a couple of yards offside as he popped up on the right-wing to blast a shot into the back of the net.

But still Posh pushed, Terry Bly was unlucky with a header which went just over the crossbar and Rayner's long shot found its way into the arms of Potter. Posh threw in everything in the closing minutes of the game, but the Villa defenders hacked away unmercifully at everything above ground level, as hopes of a last-minute equaliser by United faded.

Posh: Jack Walls, Dick Whittaker, Jim Walker, Jim Rayner, Roy Banham, Keith Ripley, Billy Hails, Dennis Emery, Terry Bly, Ray Smith, Peter McNamee.

Attendance:64,531

Posh needed two replays to finally beat Colchester United in the First Round in **1961/62**, after a 3-3 draw at London Road and 2-2 draw at Layer Road. It was on the morning of the second replay that one of Posh`s greatest-ever players, Dennis Emery suffered serious injuries when he was involved in a car crash on his way to the ground. Ray Smith replaced Dennis Emery when the match was played that evening at the neutral Carrow Road and Posh finally won 3-0, with George Hudson netting a hat-trick. They knocked out Torquay United, winning 4-1 away, in the Second Round and were then drawn away to Second Division, Newcastle United in the Third Round and they further enhanced their 'Giant Killer' tag with a 1-0 win at St James` Park against a Newcastle team that included future Posh player Brian Wright, with Terry Bly scoring the all-important goal.

Match Report

v Newcastle United, St James' Park, 3rd Round, 6th January 1962.

Newcastle United 0 Posh 1

Despite being in the 2nd Division, Newcastle United, going into this game, were the winners of more FA Cup honours in the previous decade than any other club in the country. But this didn't appear to worry Posh as they ran out 1-0 winners at St James' Park.

It could have been so different though, had Newcastle's goal on 7 minutes, scored by Ivor Allchurch stood, but the referee correctly disallowed the goal. Billy Hails had a great chance to score when left-back Bobby Ferguson missed a low cross from Roy Senior, but before he could control the ball, Newcastle keeper Dave Hollins dived to smother the ball. This let-off seemed to bring new life to Newcastle and for 20 minutes they dominated. However, Posh battled away and another shot by Hails had Hollins clutching vainly in the air, but sadly for the Posh the ball hit the crossbar.

In the second half, a shot from Roy Senior ran along the front of the bar, but Posh weren't to be denied, as a brilliantly placed through-ball from Keith Ripley split the home defence and Terry Bly ran to get to the ball before centre-half Bill Thompson, it looked as though Bly had taken the ball too far and as Hollins moved slightly to cut off an expected cross, Bly hammered in a terrific drive leaving the keeper helpless. With 17 minutes left of play, Newcastle pushed hard for an equaliser and centre forward John McGuigan missed a sitter, before the 3,000 Posh fans who had made the trip enjoyed celebrating yet another FA Cup giant-killing win.

Posh: Jack Walls, Dick Whittaker, Jim Walker, Jim Rayner, Ollie Hopkins, Keith Ripley, Billy Hails, Ray Smith, Terry Bly, George Hudson, Roy Senior.

Attendance: 42,782

First Division Sheffield United ended, the now regular, Posh cup run that year with a 3-1 win at London Road in front of a crowd of over 28,000, The Blades were 3-0 up by half-time, before George Hudson scored a second-half consolation goal for Posh, his seventh goal in that season`s FA Cup run.

George Hudson scored seven goals in Posh`s 1961/62 FA Cup run.

Notts County 3-0 away and Enfield 1-0 at home were Posh`s victims in the First and Second Rounds in **1962/63**. This earned Posh an away tie, on a frozen pitch, at Derby County in the Third Round, which The Rams won 2-0, the outstanding Posh player in the match was Dennis Emery on his return to action after 15 months following his car crash.

In **1963/64** Posh fell at the first hurdle for the first time in eight years, losing 2-1 to Watford at Vicarage Road, after extra-time, in a First Round replay, following a 1-1 draw in the original tie at London Road.

In **1964/65,** Posh`s most successful cup run began with a comfortable 5-1 home win over Salisbury City, with Derek Dougan scoring a hat-trick, they then dispatched Queen`s Park Rangers in a Second Round replay at London Road, winning 2-1 after extra-time, thanks to two Peter Deakin goals, following a 3-3 draw at Loftus Road. The Third Round saw a 3-0 away win over Chesterfield, with Derek Dougan scoring another hat-trick, although the match was overshadowed by a tragedy, as a car carrying four Chesterfield players, to watch Posh`s replay in the previous round, had been involved in a crash on the A1 and one of the four, Ralph Hunt later died from his injuries. Then came probably the greatest FA Cup victory in Posh`s history as they beat Arsenal 2-1 at London Road, in front of a crowd of over 30,000, in the Fourth Round. Posh came from behind to win with goals from Derek Dougan and the winner from Peter McNamee, whose goal sparked a celebratory pitch invasion by the Posh fans.

Match Report

v Arsenal, London Road, 4th Round, 30th January 1965.

Posh 2 Arsenal 1

Peter McNamee's goal knocked Arsenal out of the cup five minutes from the end of this breathtaking game, when Arsenal were going all out for a winner.

Arsenal had some frightening moments in the first half with Derek Dougan constantly beating Ian Ure in the air and he was inches wide of the far post with one header, from a Graham Birks free-kick. Also, in the first half Tony Burns, the Arsenal keeper, had to make a flying save from McNamee. Posh goalkeeper Willie Duff had not made a save of note, when Arsenal snatched the lead in the 43rd minute, George Eastham took a corner on the right and John Radford, on the far post, smashed in a superb goal.

Arsenal must have wondered what hit them, after seeming to take complete command in the second half. Duff made four amazing saves in the last 20 minutes, from Joe Baker (twice), Alan Skirton and Eastham. Then right-winger, Ron Barnes provided the passes for Posh to win the game. On 72 minutes, from his normal right-wing spot, Barnes sent the glitzy Irish colossus, Derek Dougan through the middle to stroke a left-footed shot wide of the advancing Arsenal keeper to make the score 1-1. Then on 85 minutes, Posh centre-half Frank Rankmore headed the ball clear to left-winger McNamee, at that point there appeared to be no danger for Arsenal, but McNamee flashed the ball out to Barnes, who had switched to the left-wing and his return pass was cracked in first time by the jubilant McNamee. After the remaining 5 minutes of play finished, Arsenal became the first and only First Division club to lose to The Posh.

Posh: Willie Duff, Ron Cooper, Graham Birks, Vic Crowe, Frank Rankmore, Harry Orr, Ron Barnes, Ollie Conmy, Derek Dougan, Peter Deakin, Peter McNamee.

Attendance: 30, 056

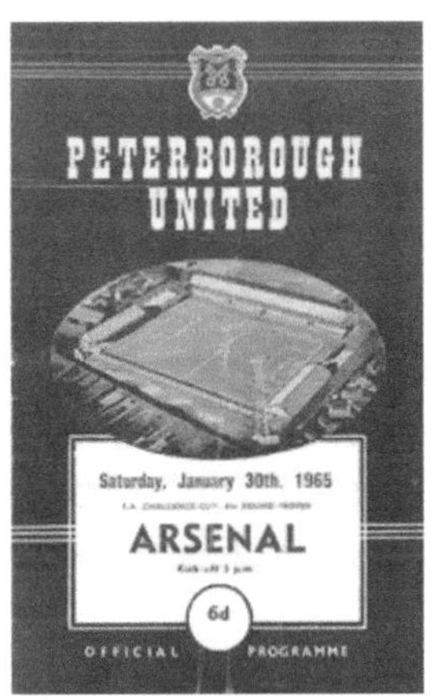

Peter McNamee scores the winning goal against Arsenal.

Posh needed a replay to see off Swansea Town (now Swansea City), with a Peter Deakin brace giving them a 2-0 win in the Fifth Round after a 0-0 draw in the first tie, which was played in front of the biggest ever crowd at London Road of 30,096. So Posh had reached the heady heights of the Sixth Round (the quarter-finals) of the FA Cup and were drawn against Chelsea at Stamford Bridge. In front of a crowd of over 63,000, Posh faced a Chelsea side, managed by Tommy Docherty, with the likes of Peter Bonnetti, Ron Harris, John Hollins, George Graham, Terry Venables and Bobby Tambling in their side. Also in the side was Bert Murray, who would become familiar to Posh fans in the years to come. Chelsea raced into a 4-0 lead before Vic Crowe, who had struggled through most of the game with an injury, in the days before substitutes, pulled a goal back for Posh. Unfortunately, Chelsea added a fifth goal and Posh`s dream ended in a 5-1 defeat and it was Chelsea who went into the semi-finals.

Match Report

v Chelsea, Stamford Bridge, 6th Round, 6th March 1965.

Chelsea 5 Posh 1

Referee Jack Parkinson had hardly put his notebook in his pocket after the toss-up, when Posh captain Vic Crowe slipped trying to make the first tackle of the game, play continued for a moment and then Crowe was taken off on a stretcher with a torn groin muscle, by the time Crowe returned to the pitch, limping badly, after 18 minutes, Chelsea were 3-0 up. Bobby Tambling screwed a ball between Willie Duff's left arm and the post for Chelsea's first. John Hollins then cracked in a goal after Marvin Hinton overran the ball at a free-kick, to let John Mortimore play it, with Hollins running through a gap, to make it 2-0. The third came with just 15 minutes on the clock, with Tambling, from the narrowest of angles, shooting calmly through Duff's legs. Duff was apprehensive and to blame for two of those goals and he might have cut off Bert Murray's centre that led to Barry Bridges getting Chelsea's fourth goal. No side can let Chelsea get away with a four-goal head start and although the limping Crowe had used his injured leg to steer a McNamee drive in to make it 4-1, there was no Posh comeback. Posh had to fight the rest of this game as a rearguard action, but can at least claim that they were never disgraced and that few teams could have done better. It wasn't until the 88th minute that Chelsea scored again, through Murray, with an overhead shot. Defeated 5-1, but Posh had reached the quarter finals of the FA Cup for the first time in the club's history and no one could take away that from them.

Posh: Willie Duff, Ron Cooper, Graham Birks, Vic Crowe, Frank Rankmore, Harry Orr, Ron Barnes, Ollie Conmy, Derek Dougan, Peter Deakin, Peter McNamee.

Attendance: 63,635

"The Doog" scored two hat-tricks in FA Cup matches in 1964/65.

Gordon Clark led his Posh side to the FA Cup Quarter-finals.

In comparison, the following season **1965/66** was a bit of an anti-climax, as Posh bowed out in the Second Round, losing 3-2 away from home to Shrewsbury Town, having beaten Kidderminster Harriers 2-1 at home in the First Round, with Peter Deakin scoring both Posh goals.

Season **1966/67**, saw some improvement as Posh progressed to the Fourth Round, beating Hereford United 4-1 at London Road in the First Round, in a game in which Peter Johnson became the first Posh player to be named as a substitute, although he was unused. Colchester United were then beaten 3-0 at Layer Road in the Second Round and Bedford Town were defeated 6-2 away in the Third Round, with Tommy Watson scoring a hat-trick. They eventually went out to Sunderland, losing 7-1 at Roker Park, where George Adams became the first player to come on as a substitute for Posh in an FA Cup tie, when he replaced Peter Johnson. This heavy defeat to Sunderland was made worse by the fact that extra bonuses offered to the players if they won the game, was one of the charges brought against Peterborough United FC by the Football Association and the Football League Commission, which ultimately led to them being demoted to the Fourth Division at the end of the following season.

Match Report

v Sunderland, Roker Park, 4th Round, 18th February 1967.

Sunderland 7 Posh 1

Despite Posh being without skipper Frank Rankmore, leading goal scorer John Fairbrother and losing Peter Johnson in the 16th minute of the game through injury, Sunderland were in a class of their own and deserved their victory.

Any hopes of a giant-killing win against First Division side Sunderland, were swept away by three goals inside five minutes, before 20 minutes had been played. John O'Hare scored with a drive from the edge of the area in the 13th minute and a minute later Cecil Irwin began a move on the right, which 17-year-old Bobby Kerr took over and from his chip Neil Martin headed Sunderland into a two-goal lead. Four minutes later Posh were out of the cup, Kerr put the ball in the net, after Posh goalkeeper Tony Millington could only parry an angled Martin shot. After a brief pause, Sunderland streaked forward again and despite Martin looking offside he flicked the ball past Millington in the 27th minute. Posh did get into the game and Ollie Conmy brought the Sunderland Under 23 international goalkeeper Jim

Continued...

Montgomery into action with a great 25-yard volley. Then Tommy Watson caught the home side napping with a low cross, but the ball hit John Kirkham's knee and went out for a goal-kick.
Within two minutes of the restart Posh were 5-0 down, after George Mulhall sent in a low cross, from which the ball slipped from Millington grasp and Martin scored his third goal of the game. On 50 minutes Kerr struck again, sending a tremendous swerving shot into the far corner of the net from 25 yards, the goal was disputed as a linesman had flagged for offside, but the referee overruled him. Posh did get a goal back in the 55th minute, when Tommy Watson curled the ball past three defenders and goalkeeper Montgomery, from 20 yards. The goal seemed to put new life into Posh and Conmy and Byrne began to create openings for the rest of the attack, but some fine saves from Montgomery, especially two from John Mason and Mike Beesley, kept the Sunderland goal intact. Sunderland were awarded a penalty in the 74th minute, after Ron Cooper brought down Martin and Jim Baxter scored from the spot, with a fierce kick into the roof of the net. Byrne then missed a sitter, after side-stepping one tackle and fooling Montgomery, he side-footed the ball the wrong side of an upright, in front of an empty net. Two saves from Millington, one from Mulhall and another from Irwin, stopped Sunderland adding more goals and even then, O'Hare hit an upright before the final whistle went.

Posh: Tony Millington, Peter Johnson (sub George Adams), Ian Crawford, Ron Cooper, John Kirkham, Brian Wright, Ollie Conmy, Tommy Watson, Mike Beesley, John Mason, Johnny Byrne.

Attendance: 43,998

In **1967/68** Posh beat non-league clubs Falmouth Town 5-2 at home and Margate 4-0 away in the first two rounds, with John Fairbrother scoring a hat-trick in the Falmouth Town match. They went out to Portsmouth, losing 1-0 at home in the Third Round.

Bristol Rovers of the Third Division dumped Posh, who were newly demoted back to the Fourth Division, out of the cup in the First Round in **1968/69**, winning 3-1 at the Eastville Stadium, with Bobby Downes scoring the Posh goal, which had given them a 1-0 lead at half-time.

Posh made it to the Fourth Round in **1969/70**, where they were beaten 5-1 by Gillingham at the Priestfield Stadium. In the previous three rounds they had beaten Falmouth Town 4-1 away, then Plymouth Argyle 2-0 at home, on a snow-covered pitch and Rotherham United 1-0 away, before bowing out at the hands of The Gills, who were in the division above Posh. The First Round match at Falmouth Town, saw Tommy Robson make the first of his club-record, 45 FA Cup appearances for Posh.

5. The 1970s

In season **1970/71**, goals from Colin Garwood, Bobby Moss and Jim Hall saw Posh beat Wimbledon, of the Southern League, 3-1 at home in the First Round, before becoming the victims of a 'giant-killing' themselves, when Wigan Athletic, who were a non-league team from the Northern Premier League at the time, won the Second Round tie 2-1 at Springfield Park. It was the first time that Posh had been beaten by a non-league team since they had joined the Football League a decade earlier.

Match Report

v Wigan Athletic, Springfield Park, 2nd Round, 12th December 1970.

Wigan Athletic 2 Posh 1

The Posh suffered a dose of their own medicine when Wigan Athletic became the first non-league team to beat Posh, as a Football League side.

Posh cannot claim to have been unlucky or even robbed, they were battered by Wigan, particularly in the first half, when they threatened to run riot. Posh's cause was not helped by the loss of John Wile, who was transferred to West Bromwich Albion on the eve of the game and the injury to player-manager Jim Iley after only ten minutes, when he was hacked down from behind and was forced to limp off to be replaced by right-winger Bobby Moss. Posh `keeper Mick Drewery made two brilliant saves from ex-Everton player Derek Temple and player-manager Gordon Milne, the former Liverpool and England player. Full-back Sutherland hit the crossbar, Temple had a goal disallowed and Davies and Fleming fluffed easy chances. Wigan eventually went ahead three minutes before the interval with a Davies header.

Posh played with more assurance and authority in the second half and Colin Garwood saw a goal-bound header cleared off the line by centre-half Coutts, with the Wigan `keeper well beaten. Then moments later, Jim Hall headed a Bob Turpie corner down and Moss scooped the ball home. A replay looked in the making until the 88th minute, when Wigan launched another attack and Brian Wright blocked Oates cross and a penalty was given. The penalty, taken by Jim Fleming was decisive, giving Drewery no chance. Chris Turner, making his FA Cup debut, did everything efficiently and can be satisfied with his performance.

Posh: Mick Drewery, Frank Noble, John Duncliffe, Jim Iley (sub Bobby Moss), Chris Turner, Brian Wright, David Pleat, Colin Garwood, Jim Hall, Bob Turpie, Tommy Robson.

Attendance:17,180

The following season **1971/72**, Posh needed a replay in the First Round to beat Redditch United, winning 6-0 in the replay at London Road following a 1-1 draw away from home, two days earlier. It was in the replay of this game, that Jim Hall became the first Posh player to be sent-off in an FA Cup match, having earlier scored two of the six Posh goals.

In the Second Round Posh beat Enfield 4-0 at home, with two goals apiece for Peter Price and Jim Hall, before going out 2-0 to First Division, Ipswich Town in the Third Round at London Road.

Season **1972/73** saw a First Round victory over Northampton Town 1-0, with Jim Hall scoring the winning goal, against his former club, in the last minute of the game.

Jim Hall scored a last-minute winner against The Cobblers.

Then in the Second Round, a 2-2 draw with non-league side Bishop`s Stortford was followed by a 3-1 win at London Road in the replay, in the Bishop`s Stortford side was future Posh manager John Still. Derby County, who were the reigning First Division champions, then knocked Posh out in the Third Round, winning 1-0 in front of a crowd of over 20,000 at London Road.

Match Report

v Derby County, London Road, 3rd Round, 13th January 1973.

Posh 0 Derby County 1

Although Posh were outplayed in the first half by the First Division champions, they hit back after the break and the Derby players were more relieved to hear the final whistle than United.

In the first minute, Derby striker Roger Davies forced a corner out on the left and it looked as if United were going to be handed an expensive lesson. England international, David Nish set the next attack in motion, with a pass to Kevin Hector who found John O'Hare, whose shot hit

Continued...

the side-netting. It took United 12 minutes to get their first real shot at goal, when Jim Hall set Don Heath free, but the winger shot wide. Then United thought they had gone ahead when Roy McFarland missed a ball and Tommy Robson sent Jim Hall racing through the middle, he rounded Colin Boulton and hit the net, however referee David Richardson blew for offside. Derby stormed back and Alan Durban blasted a 20-yarder which Mick Drewery held at the second attempt after diving to his left. Then in the 36th minute, Posh `keeper Drewery appeared to be bundled over as a corner-kick was swept over from the right, United defenders kicked two shots off the line, but Davies got to a rebound and knocked the ball into the net.

After the interval John Cozens began causing trouble and Boulton had to be at his best to keep him out in the opening minutes. United thought they deserved a penalty in the build up to Cozens' attempt, with Robson being upended, but nothing was given. Now it was County who were forced to soak up the pressure, Chris Turner set up a fine opening for Hall, the United marksman flicked the ball past Boulton, but sadly also the wrong side of the post. Heath and Hall then combined to split the Derby defence, but the cross for Cozens was cleared. With 15 minutes to go, Brian Clough replaced Davies with defender Hennessey to calm the Derby defence. Hall was involved in the last two dangerous attacks of the game, first he set up an opening for Turner, but the centre-half was penalised, then the striker himself fired a fierce 20-yarder just wide.

Posh: Mick Drewery, Keith Bradley, Jack Carmichael, John Duncliffe, Dennis Oakes, Chris Turner, Don Heath, John Cozens, Jim Hall, Eric Young, Tommy Robson (sub Ray Smith).

Attendance: 20,885

After beating Colchester United 3-2 at Layer Road in the First Round in **1973/74**, Posh then beat Wycombe Wanderers 3-1 at Loakes Park in the Second Round. Southend United were beaten 3-1 in the Third Round at London Road, with John Cozens, Freddie Hill and Tommy Robson scoring the Posh goals.

.

The three goal scorers v Southend United
Tommy Robson, Freddie Hill and John Cozens.

In the Fourth Round, Posh were drawn at home to Leeds United, who had been the winners and runners-up in the competition in the previous two seasons. A sell-out crowd of 28,000 at London Road saw Leeds, with a host of international players in their side, win the tie 4-1.

Match Report

v Leeds Utd, London Road, 4th Round, 26th January 1974.

Posh 1 Leeds United 4

Any thoughts of Posh causing one of the cup sensations of all-time were shattered in the space of 19 minutes, as Leeds scored four goals in the first half of this cup tie. With no Jack Charlton, Johnny Giles, Allan Clarke or Mick Jones, Leeds still had the quality in their 'makeshift' team to comfortably beat Posh 4-1.

Continued...

Up until Peter Lorimer's 15th minute goal though, Posh were as good as their opponents, but when referee Mr. Matthewson harshly adjudged Chris Turner's aerial challenge on Joe Jordan illegal, things went downhill for Posh. Lorimer took the free-kick and it deflected out of the reach of goalkeeper Mick Drewery off a defender. Then Joe Jordan twice lost defenders, to head home Lorimer crosses in the 24th and 30th minutes. Keith Bradley was dispossessed by Lorimer and Terry Yorath added number four with ease in the 33rd minute. To Posh's credit they went down with honour with Freddie Hill and Bert Murray showing touches of class in midfield.

Posh improved considerably in the second half and skipper John Cozens scored in the 63rd minute by heading in from Tommy Robson's cross. The fact that Bert Murray later hit an upright and Cozens had a justified penalty appeal rejected shows that Leeds never had matters all their own way, although they always gave the impression they had more in reserve if needed.

Posh: Mick Drewery, Keith Bradley, Jeff Lee, Dave Llewelyn, Chris Turner, Mick Jones, Bert Murray, John Cozens, Jim Hall (sub Jack Carmichael), Freddie Hill, Tommy Robson.

Attendance 28,000

Posh went all the way to the Fifth Round in **1974/75**, although they struggled a bit in the First Round, needing two replays to finally dispatch non-league club Weymouth, drawing 0-0 at

London Road and coming from behind three times at Weymouth`s Recreation Ground to draw 3-3, after extra-time. A toss of a coin decided the venue of the second replay would be London Road and Posh eventually went through with a 3-0 win. Posh made easier work of the next rounds, beating Charlton Athletic 3-0 at home in the Second Round, Tranmere Rovers 1-0 at home in the Third Round. Posh were drawn away to Stafford Rangers in the Fourth Round, the game created such interest that is was played at Stoke City`s Victoria Ground and attracted a crowd of over 31,000. The non-league team gave Posh a scare by taking at 10th minute lead, but goals from Jon Nixon and Dave Gregory gave Posh a 2-1 win. The Fifth Round draw gave Posh a home tie against Middlesbrough, who were managed by Jack Charlton, the tie ended in a 1-1 draw and the replay at Ayresome Park saw Middlesbrough win 2-0.

Match Report

v Middlesbrough, London Road, 5th Round, 15th February 1975.

Posh 1 Middlesbrough 1

Just a matter of inches separated Posh from another great FA Cup win. Both David Gregory and David Price came that close to knocking First Division Middlesbrough out of the cup in this game.

After an initial burst, Middlesbrough were second best for the majority of the game. The power of David Price, the skill of Freddie Hill, plus the intelligent running of Tommy Robson, David Gregory and Jon Nixon unsettled the usually well organised Middlesbrough defence. Posh took the lead on 16 minutes, with Gregory taking two defenders with him to the near post as Robson crossed, the ball came to Nixon who was completely unmarked as he slid the ball home. Posh continued to look the more dangerous side, with Robson going close and `keeper Platt dropping a centre almost to the feet of Nixon.

Posh would have almost certainly been celebrating another giant-killing act, but for goalkeeper Jim Platt, who parried away a drive from Gregory just minutes before Middlesbrough's 56th minute equaliser, Alan Foggon laid on the goal for David Mills after missing a golden opportunity himself with a low cross, after Murdoch had dispossessed Bert Murray in the centre-circle. Minutes after the Middlesbrough goal, Price had a close-range shot scrambled off the line by Willie Maddren. Apart from Eric Steele making one save at the feet of Foggon, the Posh goal never came under serious pressure again. Posh kept plugging away, but Middlesbrough's defence kept them at bay, so despite being the more effective side Posh have to do it all again at Ayresome Park.

Posh: Eric Steele, Keith Bradley, Jeff Lee, Freddie Hill, Chris Turner, Jack Carmichael, Bert Murray, David Gregory, Jon Nixon, David Price, Tommy Robson.

Unused Sub: Paul Walker

Attendance: 25,742

Match Report

v Middlesbrough, Ayresome Park, 5th Round Replay, 18th February 1975.

Middlesbrough 2 Posh 0

Posh's involvement in this year`s competition finally came to an end at Middlesbrough, after being caught napping on 11 minutes, when Foggon back-headed a Frank Spraggon chip over the advancing Eric Steele. Despite Posh defending heroically, with Jack Carmichael and Chris Turner dominant figures, Middlesbrough piled on the pressure and David Mills struck an upright before Posh eventually made their presence felt in the Middlesbrough half. Posh's most promising period came in the final minutes of the first half, when left-winger Tommy Robson missed a great chance to haul Posh back into the hunt, after he was put clear by Jon Nixon, but with goalkeeper Jim Platt narrowing the angle, he fired wide of the far post. A goal at that stage would have given Posh a tremendous psychological boost. However, from the start of the second half Middlesbrough penned Posh back again as they clung on by their fingertips. Foggon sealed Posh's fate in the 86th minute with an unstoppable volley, after substitute Paul Walker had blocked an Armstrong free-kick, Bobby Murdoch floated the ball over for Foggon to hammer home from 15 yards. It was not until the dying seconds that Posh managed to break through again, when Robson extended Platt for the only time in the match, a save which gave Posh their only corner of the game.

Posh: Eric Steele, Keith Bradley (sub Paul Walker), Jeff Lee, Freddie Hill, Chris Turner, Jack Carmichael, Bert Murray, David Gregory, Jon Nixon, David Price, Tommy Robson.

Attendance: 34,303

In the **1975/76** season, Posh eased through the early rounds, beating non-league opposition Winsford United 4-1 at home and Coventry Sporting 4-0 away at Coventry City`s Highfield Road ground, in the First and Second Rounds. The Third Round saw Posh draw 0-0 with Brian Clough`s Nottingham Forest at the City Ground on a heavy pitch, on New Year`s Day, before winning the replay at London Road 1-0, with Jon Nixon scoring the winning goal to knock out the Second Division side and add another big name club to their 'giant-killing' list.

Match Report

v Nottingham Forest, London Road, 3rd Round Replay, 7th January 1976.

Posh 1 Nottingham Forest 0

With a visit to Old Trafford to play Manchester Utd in the next round of the FA Cup at stake, both sides knew how important it was for them to win this game. With Posh £80,000 in debt, the club and the whole city knew a bumper payday from a visit to Old Trafford would be a godsend. However, for long periods in the game that prospect didn't look on the cards.

The goal that won it for Posh came after 22 minutes, when Jim Walker, who had been given permission to play by Nottingham Forest manager Brian Clough, ran down the left-wing, beat Sammy Chapman and crossed the ball to Jon Nixon, who had just returned to the pitch from the dressing room with four stitches in a knee injury, Nixon struck the ball past Peter Wells in the Forest goal, after beating Frank Clark to the cross. Posh then endured constant Forest pressure, but Chris Turner and Jack Carmichael were at their best at the heart of the Posh defence and goalkeeper Eric Steele made five good saves from Barry Butlin, Ian Bowyer, Sammy Chapman, Paul Richardson and John O'Hare. Just before the end of the game, striker David Gregory showed why so many clubs are watching him, as he beat three men inside the penalty area before flashing a shot just wide. Although it wasn't a great game, Posh tackled with courage and precision and manager Noel Cantwell said "Although it wasn't always good to watch, we deserved the win."

Manchester Utd and Old Trafford, here we come!

Posh: Eric Steele, Bert Murray, Jim Walker, Peter Eustace, Chris Turner, Jack Carmichael, Jon Nixon, David Gregory, John Cozens, Lyndon Hughes, Tommy Robson.

Unused Sub: Mick Jones

Attendance: 17,866

Jon Nixon scores the winning goal against Nottingham Forest 7th January 1976

The Fourth Round paired Posh with Manchester United, the team Posh manager Noel Cantwell had captained to victory in the 1963 FA Cup Final. Posh lost 3-1 at Old Trafford in front of 56,352, over 10,000 of whom had travelled from Peterborough, with John Cozens on target for Posh. Manchester United went on to be beaten finalists that season.

Match Report

v Manchester United, Old Trafford, 4th Round, 24th January 1976.

Manchester United 3 Posh 1

The Posh, in front of the third biggest crowd they had ever played before, exited the cup at Old Trafford with pride and dignity.

Despite being 2-0 down after just 10 minutes, Posh never crumbled and put in a brave and bold performance. Both early goals were unfortunate, the first came in the 7th minute when Alex Forsyth's fierce drive was unluckily deflected by Chris Turner out of the reach of Posh keeper Eric Steele and then just three minutes later Gordon Hill chipped across for Sammy McIlroy to head in, with Stuart Pearson appearing to be in an offside position when starting the move. So, after 10 minutes and with the Stretford End expecting a cricket score, Posh showed their character and ability, as the team's performance shone through in the face of adversity. Posh created as many, if not more, clear-cut chances and had one of those been tucked away then who knows what the outcome might have been. Cozens sent one header straight at goalkeeper Alex Stepney, shortly after reducing the arrears in the 35th minute, when he coolly made the most of a Brian Greenhoff slip.

United always had the extra yard of pace and an abundance of skills on the flanks in Hill and Steve Coppell, but in the early stages of the second half Posh were taking the tie to United. In the early moments of the second period, both Cozens and Jon Nixon had opportunities in the same raid, to have thrown the tie back into the melting pot. It took a world class goal from Gordon Hill, blasting home from 25 yards, to steady the less than comfortable United in the 68th minute. Late on, The Red Devils adopted time-wasting tactics much to the annoyance of their own supporters, which must have shown how shaken they had been by Posh's efforts.

Posh: Eric Steele, Bert Murray, Jim Walker, Peter Eustace, Chris Turner, Jack Carmichael, Jon Nixon, David Gregory, John Cozens, Lyndon Hughes, Tommy Robson (sub Mick Jones)

Attendance: 56,352

Noel Cantwell managed Posh against his former club Manchester United.

Season **1976/77** saw Tranmere Rovers beaten 4-0 at Prenton Park in the First Round. The Second Round tie away against Northwich Victoria was abandoned after 24 minutes due to heavy fog in Cheshire, with Posh leading 1-0. In the rearranged match, Posh suffered the indignity of being knocked out by a non-league club for the second time since gaining league status themselves and they were well and truly beaten, losing 4-0!

Match Report

v Northwich Victoria, Drill Field, 2nd Round, 14th December 1976.
Northwich Victoria 4 Posh 0

Despite leading 1-0 in the original game that was abandoned due to fog, Posh never reproduced any of that form and were totally humiliated, as they were thrashed 4-0 by Northern Premier League side Northwich Victoria.

Northwich took the lead, ironically in the 24th minute (the exact time the first game was abandoned) through centre-forward Phil Smith, who with acres of room accepted a pass from Phil Jones and hammered the ball past Keith Waugh from close range.

Bob Doyle had a fine game in midfield, prompting almost all of Posh's more promising moves and it was he who began to open Northwich up in the second half. Twice he got into threatening positions, but was fouled by Albre Nieman and Phil Jones, both of whom had

Continued...

their names taken.
Posh were persistently applying pressure when Northwich scored their second goal on 62 minutes, against the run of play. Smith took possession and ran the ball just inside the Posh box, when Derek Jefferies tackled him and the Northwich player fell awkwardly, the linesman flagged and referee Lowe immediately awarded a penalty, Wain duly planted the spot-kick home.
Straight away Posh substituted Keith Oakes for David Gregory and things began to happen. Gregory sent John Cozens through for Posh's best chance of the match, but ex-Stoke keeper John Farmer came flying out to turn his shot around the post.
This was the end of Peterborough, for Northwich went away to score their third goal on 82 minutes, when midfield star Johnny King found Jeff Swede with a great through-ball. Swede took the ball on, then beat Waugh with a well-placed low shot. Smith rubbed salt in the wounds when, in the last minute, he rose high to head in a perfect cross from Swede.
Posh: Keith Waugh, Peter Hindley, Keith Oakes (sub David Gregory), Bob Doyle, Chris Turner, Derek Jefferies, Jack Carmichael, Jon Nixon, Ernie Moss, John Cozens, Tommy Robson.

Attendance: 5,070

In **1977/78**, Posh beat non-league Barnet 2-1, at Underhill in the First Round. Barnet had ex-England forward Jimmy Greaves and ex-Posh forward John Fairbrother in their line-up. Then in the Second Round, they knocked out Gillingham at the second attempt, after drawing 1-1 away, they won the replay at London Road 2-0. In the Third Round they held Newcastle United to a 1-1 draw at London Road and came close to an upset. In the replay at St James` Park, Posh put up a brave performance, but in the end the windy conditions and the quality of the opposition were too much for them and The Magpies won 2-0.

Match Report

v Newcastle United, London Road, 3rd Round, 7th January 1978.

Posh 1 Newcastle United 1

A bumper crowd of 17,621 were treated to a cracking game of football, in a match that had everything except a winning goal.

Posh made an excellent start to the tie, but in the 21st minute Newcastle midfielder Ray Hudson charged forward and hit a left-foot volley from 18 yards, that sent Posh keeper Jim Barron the wrong way, with the aid of a deflection. But the setback prompted Posh to tear into attack and they equalised just six minutes later, when an Ian Ross free-kick was headed across the goal by Chris Turner, Gary Sargent rose and with considerable cool, nodded the ball past Magpies keeper Carr. Tommy Robson gave Ray Blackhall a nightmare match, the Newcastle defender was repeatedly turned inside-out by the veteran Posh winger, who seemed to revel in performing against his old club.

There was a tremendous spell in the second half when Posh had Newcastle on the rack, in fact, on two occasions Posh might have felt justified in claiming a penalty, when first Billy McEwan and then Jeff Lee were flattened in the area. Posh fans thought a replay wasn't necessary, as Jack Carmichael headed the ball home late in the second half, but referee Derek Turner silenced the Posh fans by penalising Tommy Robson for impeding young goalkeeper Kevin Carr, as Gary Sargent's looping cross came over. In the dying minutes, Turner headed a free-kick over the bar and Robson broke through a couple of times, but it turned out that Posh must travel to St James' Park for a replay.

Posh: Jim Barron, Lyndon Hughes, Jeff Lee, Bob Doyle, Chris Turner, Ian Ross, Alan Slough, Gary Sargent, Tommy Robson, Billy McEwan, Jack Carmichael.

Unused sub: Keith Oakes.

Attendance: 17,621

Match Report

v Newcastle United, St James` Park, 3rd Round Replay, 11th January 1978.

Newcastle United 2 Posh 0

As Posh's First Division opponents had been lucky to get a draw in the first game in this round of the cup, skipper Chris Turner chose, after winning the toss, to play the first half against the howling wind.

Continued...

Newcastle tried all sorts of tactics, short passes, long passes, shots, but apart from two Tommy Craig efforts and an Irving Nattrass effort Posh weathered the storm well. Jim Barron saved well from Tommy Craig in the 7th minute and again just before half-time, when he went full-stretch to foil him once more. Nattrass struck the post with a fierce drive, but no one else in the Newcastle side looked like scoring in the first half.

In the second half, with the wind at their backs, Posh should have been on the offensive, but just four minutes into the half Ian Ross, under pressure under-hit a pass to goalkeeper Barron and Ray Hudson was brought down by a late challenge by Jack Carmichael in the penalty-area, Tommy Craig made no mistake from the penalty-spot and Posh were trailing 1-0, now with a mountain to climb. Despite their tag of cup fighters, Posh did not live up to that reputation and Newcastle grew in confidence. Despite a couple of Posh shots, there was not to be another Posh cup upset. In the 86th minute Mickey Burns, from the right, sent the ball over to Ray Blackhall who, 20 yards out, hammered it first-time past Barron.

Posh: Jim Barron, Lyndon Hughes, Jeff Lee, Bob Doyle, Chris Turner, Ian Ross, Alan Slough, Gary Sargent, Tommy Robson, Billy McEwan, Jack Carmichael.

Unused sub: Keith Oakes.

Attendance: 25,770

The usual good cup run failed to materialise for Posh in **1978/79** as they lost 3-2 away to Southend United in the First Round, with Trevor Anderson and Barry Butlin scoring the Posh goals.

The following season, **1979/80** was no better as AFC Bournemouth came to London Road in the First Round and left with a 2-1 win, with Billy Kellock the goal scorer for Posh.

6. The 1980s

After a disappointing end to the Seventies for Posh in the cup, things returned to normal as the Eighties began, in season **1980/81**, Posh beat Northampton Town 4-1 at the County Ground in the First Round. They then beat Barnet, with ex-Posh player Gary Sargent in their side, 1-0 away in the Second Round. Chesterfield held Posh to a 1-1 draw at London Road in the Third Round, before Posh won the replay 2-1, with Robbie Cooke scoring all three Posh goals over the two ties. Notts County, from two divisions above Posh and sitting on top of their league, were next to fall by the wayside as Posh won 1-0, thanks to another Robbie Cooke goal, at Meadow Lane in the Fourth Round to earn a home tie with Manchester City in the Fifth Round.

A narrow 1-0 win for City, who went on to be beaten in the final by Tottenham Hotspur, ended the FA Cup dream for Posh for another season, in front of a near full-house at London Road. It was in this game that the great Tommy Robson made the last of his incredible 45 FA Cup appearances for The Posh.

Match Report

v Manchester City, London Road, 5th Round, 14th February 1981.

Posh 0 Manchester City 1

Although beaten, Posh were not disgraced by First Division Manchester City in this 5th Round tie. A single goal, scored by Manchester City defender Tommy Booth in the 42nd minute, decided the issue.

Posh had plenty of chances in the first half, the first of which came in the first minute of the game, when Micky Gynn ran with the ball from the centre-circle to the City 18-yard box, however the ball didn't bounce kindly and the chance was gone. Posh had another chance to open the scoring in the 10th minute, after a lovely turn and chip by Tommy Robson saw Robbie Cooke head just wide. Robson might have scored two minutes later, when Cooke returned the compliment by flicking on a Gordon Hodgson free-kick. After half an hour Robson broke on the right and crossed well to Kellock, who headed just wide. Five minutes later, Kellock chipped the ball over Booth to leave Cooke clear, but he put it well over. City had certainly been outshone during these early stages, but not completely stifled. Their captain, Paul Power had been willing to run at defenders and Tommy Hutchinson, given a free role by City, popped up on both wings and always got his cross in. City full-back Tony Henry almost scored an own-goal when, after Gynn had run through, he took the ball off him and turned it back to Joe Corrigan only to find he was not there, the goalkeeper had moved across to cover an expected shot but managed to recover the ball in time. This appeared to wake up City, as they began to apply more pressure on Posh. City had the ball in the net after 40 minutes, when Kevin Reeves flicked on a corner for Dave Bennett to shoot, the ball was blocked by McDonald, who scooped it into the net with his hand, fortunately the referee saw it and disallowed the goal. However, a minute later City did score and this one stood, Tommy Hutchinson's corner was only half-cleared, Power shot and although his effort was blocked, the ball spun free to Booth who stroked it home. Posh still had another chance before the interval to score when Robson crossed but Kellock again headed just wide.

The second half was a completely different story. City took a grip on the game and Posh's only real chance of the half came from a free-kick that Kellock hit just over.

Posh: Keith Waugh, Dave McVay, Ian Phillips (sub Dave Syrett), Micky Gynn, Trevor Slack, Alan Slough, Trevor Quow, Billy Kellock, Robbie Cooke, Gordon Hodgson, Tommy Robson.

Attendance: 27,780

Tommy Robson made more FA Cup appearances for Posh than any other player.

Posh captain Billy Kellock (No.8) prior to the Fifth Round tie against Manchester City at London Road.

1981/82 saw Posh progress to the Third Round by beating Halifax Town 3-0 away in the First Round and Walsall 2-1 at home in the Second Round, before losing 1-0 to Third Division side Bristol City at London Road and missing out on a glamour tie against League Champions Aston Villa, had they beaten The Robins.

In the **1982/83** season it was the Third Round again for Posh. They needed a replay to beat Chesterfield in the First Round, winning 2-1 at London Road, after a 2-2 draw in the first tie. Their passage through the Second Round was easier, as they beat Third Division side Doncaster Rovers 5-2 at London Road, with two Robbie Cooke goals, taking his total FA Cup goals for Posh to double figures.

Match Report

v Doncaster Rovers, London Road, 2nd Round, 11th December 1982.

Posh 5 Doncaster Rovers 2

Posh shrugged off their mediocre league form to impressively beat Third Division side, Doncaster Rovers at London Road, after going a goal down.

Doncaster took the lead after just three minutes, when Ian Snodin scored from close range. Micky Gynn and Robbie Cooke forced Doncaster's goalkeeper Dennis Peacock into making point-blank saves, before Cooke eventually took the ball round him and saw his shot cleared off the line by Clive Wiggington. Peterborough's onslaught eventually came to fruition, when Trevor Quow released Robbie Cooke and he made no mistake with a cross-shot which went in off the far post. Posh went into the half-time break a goal to the good after Quow intelligently found Ian Benjamin and his near-post cross was turned in by Colin Clarke. Almost straight after the restart, Cooke hit the post with a lofted shot and Clarke missed the rebound. In the 69th minute Clarke sent over a long cross, which was headed neatly in by Quow to make the score 3-1. Three minutes later, Cooke put his side 4-1 ahead when he placed a through ball from Billy Rodaway, over Peacock. Doncaster substitute Stewart Mell volleyed a spectacular consolation with three minutes left, but Micky Gynn went on to hit the fifth goal, when he wriggled into the penalty-area and hit the ball straight into the net.

Posh: David Seaman, John Winters, Steve Collins, Micky Gynn, Neil Firm, Trevor Slack, Colin Clarke, Billy Rodaway, Robbie Cooke, Ian Benjamin, Trevor Quow.

Unused sub: Ivor Linton.

Attendance: 4,012

The Third Round paired Posh with Luton Town, who were a top-flight club at the time, away at Kenilworth Road, The Hatters won comfortably, 3-0.

In the **1983/84** season, Posh fell at the first hurdle, losing 2-0 to Oxford United at the Manor Ground.

Although they made it to the Second Round in **1984/85**, it was another disappointing FA Cup season for Posh, despite the joy of beating local rivals Cambridge United 2-0 at the Abbey Stadium, thanks to two goals from Errington Kelly, in the First Round. They went out to non-league opposition for the only the third time since joining the Football League, this time in the shape of Dagenham, losing 1-0 in the Second Round, in a game which was marred by crowd trouble and the collapse of a wall, injuring a number of fans. Posh also called for an FA enquiry as the referee appeared to end the game early, but the result stood.

Match Report

v Dagenham, Victoria Road, 2nd Round, 8th December 1984.

Dagenham 1 Posh 0

This game will be remembered for controversy and sadly crowd trouble, as Dagenham became the third non-league club to knock Posh out of the FA Cup since they became members of the Football League back in 1960. The second half was delayed after fighting had broken out behind one of the goals, then a wall collapsed causing injury to fans and forcing others on to the pitch, plus the game reportedly only lasted 86 minutes!

Although Posh had more of the play, they created very few chances and although Dagenham created even less, they did find the back of the net. Both defences played well, with John Wile and Trevor Slack giving the Dagenham forwards little chance, whilst in the determined home defence Alan Campbell was outstanding. Posh's first real chance came in the 11th minute, when Kelly's cross was knocked on by Kenny Beech to Trevor Quow, but his header lacked power. Quow headed wide minutes later, as did Billy Lansdowne at the other end. Two minutes after the interval, Joe Dunwell lobbed over John Turner following a Chris Kinnear pass, to put Dagenham 1-0 up.

Four minutes after the goal, the Posh team were asked to leave the pitch by the referee, for four minutes, after the collapse of a wall. When play resumed Kenny Beech shot wide after Scott had missed a Holmes cross, Bryan Klug was off target following a Wile knock-down and Kelly put and effort the wrong side of a post after being put through by Martin Pike. Kelly came closest to scoring for Posh in the 65th minute when Phil Chard found him, but his shot bounced off the underside of the bar and to safety.

Continued...

When the final whistle went, according to watches in the Press box, the referee had played four minutes short, the time which had lapsed while Posh were off the field. Some might say Posh were robbed of the chance of a win by not playing those missing four minutes, but having created so few chances in 86 minutes it was highly unlikely that they would have scored had they played even longer than another four minutes.

Posh: John Turner, Phil Chard, Martin Pike, Kenny Beech, John Wile, Trevor Slack, Bryan Klug, Errington Kelly, Trevor Quow, Gary Worrall, Jimmy Holmes.

Unused sub: Francis Cassidy.

Attendance: 3,302

The good times returned for Posh the following season, **1985/86**. After a 2-2 draw away at Bishop`s Stortford, they won the First Round replay 3-1. Bath City were beaten 1-0 at London Road in the Second Round, before Fourth Division Posh became 'giant killers' once more. Second Division Leeds United, managed by Billy Bremner, were not the force they once had been, but even so, a 1-0 win for Posh in the Third Round, thanks to a Greig Shepherd goal, was a fantastic result, in a match that both sides ended with 10 men, Posh due to an injury to goalkeeper John Turner, with left-back Martin Pike deputising in goal and Leeds through a sending-off.

Match Report

v Leeds Utd, London Road, 3rd Round, 4th January 1986.

Posh 1 Leeds United 0

The Posh restored their reputation of cup giant-killers, beating 2nd Division side, Leeds Utd on a bone-hard, rutted and snowy London Road pitch.

Posh's Francis Cassidy was handed the best opportunity to break the deadlock in the 5th minute and despite being clear, he shot straight at Day. Leeds though, gradually began to take the initiative and a probing run by full-back Dennis Irwin finished in a low cross, which was hammered home by Scott Sellars. only to be ruled offside. Substitute, Greig Shepherd was called into action after 26 minutes, when Errington Kelly went off injured and the substitute's performance shone through in the arctic-like conditions.

It was fitting that Shepherd stole the glory with his second-half header, following a volleyed cross from Francis Cassidy in the 67th minute. Three minutes later came the only black spot of the day, when Posh goalkeeper John Tuner sustained a broken leg after being felled in a collision with former Manchester Utd forward Andy Ritchie. With Turner being whisked off to hospital, left-back Martin Pike took over in goal and Posh were down to 10 men. John Wile, making his umpteenth comeback and failing to show his age at 38, led the back four by example and Lil Fuccillo was grafting hard as he refused to let the younger Leeds

Continued...

midfielders get the better of him. The final ten minutes were frantic and Leeds midfielder Scott Sellars got himself sent-off in the 86th minute by referee Peter Tyldesley, after he scored and again the goal was disallowed. He was so angered by the linesman's decision that it earned him a booking and after more words with referee Peter Tyldesey he got his marching orders. The excitement hadn't finished yet though, as with virtually the last kick of the match Andy Ritchie drove the ball against the top of the bar from 20 yards.

Posh: John Turner, Alan Paris, Martin Pike, Francis Cassidy, John Wile, Trevor Slack, Andy Kowalski, Lil Fuccillo, Jackie Gallagher, Errington Kelly (sub Greig Shepherd), Garry Worrall.

Attendance: 10,137

Carlisle United, also of Division Two, were the Fourth Round opposition at London Road and were duly beaten 1-0, with Greig Shepherd again scoring the goal to earn Posh a Fifth Round home tie against Brighton & Hove Albion, yet another Second Division side. The match ended 2-2, so Posh travelled to the Goldstone Ground for the replay, only to lose 1-0.

Greig Shepherd scored three goals in Posh`s 1985/86 FA Cup run.

Match Report

v Brighton & Hove Albion, London Road, 5th Round, 15th February 1986.

Posh 2 Brighton & Hove Albion 2

What a day for the Posh, their best crowd for five years, record gate receipts and a performance which deserved a place in the last eight of the cup.

The game had an electrifying start, as in the opening minutes, a through ball sent Grieg Shepherd clear, he slipped the ball past Brighton keeper Perry Digweed for a certain goal, but was tripped by the keeper a yard outside of the box, referee Joe Worrall decided a booking was sufficient, which Posh felt hard done by, as earlier in the season John Turner was sent-off for a similar offence. Sadly, Posh didn't capitalise on the free-kick, but the incident appeared to unnerve Digweed, who made several mistakes, as Posh piled on the pressure. However, the keeper came to the rescue in the 34th minute, when centre-half Trevor Slack played a neat one-two with Shepherd and Digweed blocked the resulting shot from point-blank range.

The game really came to life in a 10-minute spell in the second half. Firstly, in the 73rd minute, when Shepherd rose to power home a header from Garry Worrall's free-kick. However, the Posh cheers were stifled within 90 seconds, as Brighton struck back with a Dean Saunders goal, that had more than a hint of offside about it. But back came Posh, there looked no danger when Kelly got the better of Eric Young in an aerial dual and took a speculative 25-yard ground shot in the 78th minute, Digweed sprawled to his right but could only look upwards in agony as the ball rocketed off a divot and rose six feet into the net. It may have been lucky, but just as lucky was Brighton's equaliser, a deflection off right-back Alan Paris on 83 minutes, Jacobs miscued his shot on the edge of the area, but his frustration turned to delight as the ball bobbled into the net.

Posh: Mike Astbury, Alan Paris, Martin Pike, Francis Cassidy, John Wile, Trevor Slack, Andy Kowalski, Lil Fuccillo, Errington Kelly, Greig Shepherd, Garry Worrall.

Unused sub: Jackie Gallagher.

Attendance: 15,812

Probably the less said about the **1986/87** season, the better, as Posh went out in the First Round and to make matters worse, it was away to bitter rivals Northampton Town, with The Cobblers winning 3-0.

Moving on to **1987/88**, Cardiff City were beaten 2-1 at London Road, in the First Round, with Mick Gooding scoring both goals, but Posh suffered the humiliation of being beaten 3-1 by non-league Sutton United at London Road in the Second Round, the first time Posh had lost at home to non-league opposition, since becoming a Football League club themselves.

Match Report

v Sutton Utd, London Road, 2nd Round, 5th December 1987.

Posh 1 Sutton United 3

What a shambles. Playing their 100th FA Cup tie since joining the Football League, Posh showed little passion as they were humbled by hard-working, non-league side Sutton Utd. The GM Vauxhall Conference side cost less than £5,000 to assemble, yet out played The Posh.

With only 13 fit players and without the suspended Mick Gooding, Posh were always going to find it difficult and were 1-0 down after just 5 minutes when Les Lawrence scored with a cracking header, but unfortunately it was in his own net. However, two minutes later things looked better for Posh as Lawrence redeemed himself by scoring Posh's equaliser. But, that was as good as it got for the Posh and it came as no surprise when Cornwell made it 2-1 to Sutton, in the 36th minute.

After the interval Posh's fate was sealed, when Golley scored Sutton's third goal, in the 69th minute, to make it 3-1. This was the first time Posh had lost to non-league opposition at London Road since they were elected to the Football League in 1960. After the match it came as no surprise that manager Noel Cantwell raided the transfer market to boost his side`s strike force, with two loan signings.

Posh: Joe Neenan, Alan Paris, Steve Collins (sub Mick Nuttell), Mark Nightingale, Bryn Gunn, Paul Price, Errington Kelly (sub Ashley Carr), Mick Halsall, Les Lawrence, Steve Phillips, Noel Luke.

Attendance: 4,723

Season **1988/89** saw Dave Longhurst score a hat-trick as Posh drew 3-3 away at Gillingham in the First Round, before winning the replay 1-0, after extra-time. The Second Round also required a replay, after a 0-0 draw with Brentford at London Road, Posh went out of the competition, losing 3-2 in the replay.

For the third season running, Posh failed to make it past the Second Round, in **1989/90**. They beat non-league Hayes 1-0 in a First Round replay, after being held to a 1-1 draw at London Road in the original tie. Swansea City then knocked Posh out in the Second Round, winning 3-1 at Vetch Field.

7. The 1990s

Posh drew 1-1 with Hereford United at Edgar Street in the First Round in **1990/91**, before winning the replay 2-1. The Second Round also saw Posh requiring a replay to progress past Wycombe Wanderers, after a 1-1 draw at Adams Park, where Posh were reduced to ten men when Gerry McElhinney was sent off, Posh won the replay 2-0, but were then beaten 2-1 by Port Vale, at Vale Park in the Third Round.

In the First Round in the **1991/92** season, Posh beat Harlow Town 7-0 at home, scoring six of their goals in the first-half.

Match Report

v Harlow Town, London Road, 1st Round, 16th November 1991.

Posh 7 Harlow Town 0

With Posh playing against 10 men for almost 75 minutes, this was a one-sided affair which Posh could have won by even more goals.

Posh's first goal came in the 6th minute from Gary Cooper's left foot, after David Riley controlled and played the ball to him. The second goal was a penalty scored by Gary Cooper, after referee Ray Biggar decided Gleeson had fouled Riley, though it looked as though the defender had made contact with the ball before Riley went down. Just a minute after the penalty, a long clearance by Posh keeper Barber evaded the Harlow defence and David Riley scored, beating the advancing Harlow keeper David Mallett. On 23 minutes Worrell Sterling sent a left-foot shot crashing into the net from the edge of the penalty area. Then four minutes later, Ken Charlery put Mick Halsall clear through and his shot from the edge of the penalty area went into the corner of the net. On 39 minutes a cross from the left from Gary Kimble was headed home by Charlery, despite a brave attempt by the goalkeeper to prevent the ball crossing the line.

At half time Harlow changed their defensive set-up, but it was Dave Mallett who prevented even more goals in the second half, making at least five crucial saves. Posh did score again in the 87th minute, when Garry Butterworth sent Paul Culpin clear down the left and he swerved a left-foot shot from the edge of the penalty area beyond the reach of the goalkeeper and into the far corner.

Posh: Fred Barber, Noel Luke, Peter Johnson, Mick Halsall, Dave Robinson, Steve Welsh, Worrell Sterling (sub Garry Butterworth), Gary Cooper, David Riley (sub Paul Culpin), Ken Charlery, Gary Kimble.

Attendance: 4,341

They were drawn against Reading in the Second Round, the match at London Road ended goalless, with The Royals, who had former Posh favourite Mick Gooding in their side, winning the replay 1-0.

Mick Gooding played both for and against Posh in the FA Cup.

1992/93 was a memorable season for Posh in the FA Cup, but for all the wrong reasons. They were drawn against non-league Kingstonian in the First Round and were held to a 1-1 draw at Kingsmeadow. The replay at London Road ended in what would have been a record-equalling 9-1 win, but the result was wiped from the record books and the match ordered to be replayed behind-closed-doors, following an incident in which a coin, thrown from behind the goal in the London Road End, struck the Kingstonian goalkeeper on the head and he was unable to continue. Posh went on to win the second replay 1-0. When they went out, losing 3-2 away to Plymouth Argyle in the next round, it ended a sorry episode in Posh`s otherwise distinguished FA Cup history.

Match Report

v Kingstonian, London Road, 1st Round Replay, 25th November 1992.
Posh 9 Kingstonian 1 (Result Void)

Sadly, this record-equalling FA Cup victory never was, after Kingstonian keeper Adrian Blake was struck by an object thrown by a hooligan from the London Road Terrace and the 9-1 result and Tony Philliskirk's five-goal feat was erased from the records, following the FA Disciplinary Committee`s decision to order the game to be replayed. Posh had gone 1-0 up in the 8th minute when Tony Philliskirk dived and headed Worrell Sterling's corner into the net. But for Darren Bradshaw it could have been 1-1 when Posh goalkeeper Ian Bennett's kick was charged down by David Harlow, but Bradshaw walked the ball clear. Goal number two for the Posh came in the 25th minute, with a Sterling cross directed into the net by a Philliskirk left-foot volley. Four minutes before the interval Tony Adcock netted goal number three, with a diving header from yet another Sterling cross.

Goal four came on 63 minutes, when Sterling's left-wing corner was headed on by Howarth and Adcock stole in and slotted the ball home. On 66 minutes Sterling, set free by Marcus Ebdon, squared the ball to Philliskirk who fired home a left foot shot from 16 yards to make it 5-0. Kingstonian scored the best goal of the game, when full-back John Finch blasted home from 30 yards on 73 minutes, to make it 5-1. On 82 minutes Gary Cooper scored Posh's sixth goal from 20 yards after a loose ball broke to him. Then on 86 minutes Dominic Iorfa crossed the ball which was deflected past replacement goalkeeper Andy Parr by Kingstonian midfielder David Harlow. Posh added an eighth goal on 88 minutes when Adcock broke clear from the right and Philliskirk charged down an attempted clearance and put the ball into the back of the net. The final Posh goal came in the last minute of the game after substitute Bobby Barnes pulled the ball back for Philliskirk to score from close range.

Posh: Ian Bennett, Darren Bradshaw, Ronnie Robinson, Dominic Iorfa, Lee Howarth, Steve Welsh, Worrell Sterling (sub Bobby Barnes), Gary Cooper, Tony Adcock, Tony Philliskirk, Marcus Ebdon.

Unused sub: Noel Luke.

Attendance: 5,307

Match Report

v Kingstonian, London Road, 1st Round Replay, 4th December 1992.
Posh 1 Kingstonian 0

The game no spectators saw and neither manager wanted to play.

Behind closed doors and in silence, Posh overcame a tricky pitch and a well organised defence to go through to the 2nd Round of the cup, after winning 1-0. Posh deserved to win more comfortably, spending virtually the whole of the match in the Kingstonian half and striking the woodwork twice, but credit to Kingstonian who defended with skill and in numbers, with goalkeeper Adrian Blake's handling and positional play exceptional. Blake's best moment came in first-half injury-time, when Tony Philliskirk's header from a Gary Cooper cross looked destined for the bottom corner. He will also remember his second-half stops from Worrell Sterling and Tony Adcock.

Continued...

Skipper, Steve Welsh was only denied the first goal of his professional career by the width of a post, straight after the restart. It was Sterling who finally broke the deadlock midway through the second half, from Philliskirk's cross from the left, the little winger arrived late and stooped low to head into the corner. The irony of scoring his first home goal of the season when no-one was watching wasn't lost on a smiling Sterling. Philliskirk went on to rattle the crossbar from close range ten minutes from time.
Kingstonian's best effort came on the hour when Darren Brathwaite spotted Ian Bennett off his line and tried to lob him, but from about 60 yards his effort failed.

Posh: Ian Bennett, Darren Bradshaw, Ronnie Robinson, Mick Halsall, Lee Howarth (sub Noel Luke), Steve Welsh, Worrell Sterling, Gary Cooper, Tony Adcock, Tony Philliskirk, Marcus Ebdon.

Unused sub: Dominic Iorfa.

Attendance: 0 (Played behind closed doors)

With Posh now in the second tier of the Football League, they were now themselves classed as the 'big boys' and didn`t have to join the competition until the Third Round. In **1993/94**, the draw paired them with Tottenham Hotspur at London Road, where Posh held the Premier League side to a 1-1 draw, having taken the lead through a Jason Brissett goal. In the replay at White Hart Lane, Posh again held Spurs to a 1-1 draw after extra time, this time Ken Charlery was the Posh goalscorer, but they suffered the heartbreak of losing 5-4 on penalties.

Match Report

v Tottenham Hotspur, London Road, 3rd Round, 8th January 1994.

Posh 1 Tottenham Hotspur 1

Posh came within four minutes of capturing another giant-killing scalp in the FA Cup, but have to wait until their trip to White Hart Lane to see if they can progress to the 4th Round of the cup.

Spurs started brightly and had endless first-half possession, but apart from Fred Barber making a double save from Dozzell and Anderton they failed to make any real goal-scoring opportunities. Posh had to re-organise their defence after 30 minutes, when Darren Bradshaw went off injured and fortunately Chris Greenman linked effectively with Steve Welsh at the heart of the back four while David McDonald and Ian Carter performed solidly on either side. The danger from Spurs came from Darren Anderton on the wing, but his shooting and crossing was poor.

The second half was a different kettle of fish. Posh bridged the gap in class between the two sides through persistent defending and speedy striking. Barber watched several second-half efforts from Anderton and subsitute Sol Campbell, whizz past his posts, but the arrival of Dominic Iorfa as a substitute for Tony Philliskirk prompted several anxious moments for Spurs. Posh scored within minutes of the substitution, when Iorfa's square ball was floated to the far post by Tony Adcock for Jason Brissett to drill home. It looked as though Posh would increase their lead with 5 minutes to go but Erik Thorstvedt saved goalbound shots from both Ken Charlery and Steve Welsh. Then in the 86th minute, a right-wing cross from David Kerslake was headed home by Jason Dozzell. Despite the goal Posh didn't give up and Charlery could have won it before the end, but once again Thorstvedt came to the rescue for Spurs saving his shot, after Sedgley had been fooled by some fancy footwork.

Posh: Fred Barber, David McDonald, Ian Carter, Darren Bradshaw (sub Ken Charlery), Chris Greenman, Steve Welsh, Tony Adcock, Detzi Kruszynski, Tony Philliskirk (sub Dominic Iorfa), Jason Brissett, Marcus Ebdon.

Unused sub: Mark Tyler.

Attendance: 19,169

Match Report

v Tottenham Hotspur, White Hart Lane, 3rd Round Replay, 19th January 1994.

Tottenham Hotspur 1 Posh 1 (AET) (Spurs won 5-4 on penalties)

Denied by a goalkeeper's fingertips, Posh put in a stunning performance worthy of a place in the Fourth Round, however a penalty save by Ian Walker from 16-year-old Andy Furnell knocked Posh out of the cup.

The game was not one-way traffic, Posh may have been the underdogs but they played with plenty of aggression and created the better chances. Spurs took the lead in the 12th minute when Posh keeper Fred Barber dropped the ball at Nick Barmby's feet, though Barber twice redeemed himself with brave blocks in the first half. Posh equalised in the 24th minute through Ken Charlery, in a half which was very even though Spurs enjoyed control towards the end.

Jason Brissett and Dominic Iorfa caused the Spurs defence to panic through their pace and so did Furnell, a half-time substitute for the hamstring injured Dominic Iorfa. Both Furnell and

Continued...

Charlery missed great chances to avoid the penalty shoot-out, but both missed their opportunity to score. Lee Howarth was dominant in defence and Chris Greenman played the best he had ever done in a Posh shirt. The difference in the characters of the managers at full-time was massive, with Posh`s Chris Turner walking around joking with anyone in sight, whereas Ossie Ardiles puffed nervously on an endless stream of cigarettes.
In the penalty shoot-out Posh went first with Tony Adcock, Ken Charlery and Detzi Kruszynski all scoring, Andy Furnell, penalty taker number four for Posh, had his spot-kick saved, Chris Greenman then scored his spot-kick. So, it was left for Steve Sedgley to score with his left foot, to win it for Spurs.

Posh: Fred Barber, David McDonald, Chris Greenman, John McGlashan (sub Tony Spearing), Lee Howarth, Steve Welsh, Tony Adcock, Detzi Kruszynski, Dominic Iorfa (sub Andy Furnell), Jason Brissett, Ken Charlery.
Unused sub: Mark Tyler.

Attendance: 24,893

Back in the Second Division in **1994/95**, Posh were back to entering the competition at the First Round stage. That season saw them drawn against both of their local rivals. Firstly, Northampton Town in the First Round at London Road, who they beat soundly, 4-0.

Match Report

v Northampton Town, London Road, 1st Round, 12th November 1994.
Posh 4 Northampton Town 0

Four Posh goals in the final 19 minutes of this game were in complete contrast to what had gone on before, but meant Posh were in the hat for next round of the cup.
Posh defended well, particularly in the first half, against a spirited Northampton side who attacked with style in the final quarter of the pitch. Substitute David Morrison was called into action after just 9 minutes, as Sean Farrell strained himself taking a throw-in and for much of the opening half it looked a poor swap. The substitute stayed on the edge of the action, while Farrell`s presence was sorely missed, under a stream of high crosses. In contrast Northampton's football was neat and inventive with Scott Cooksey making two fingertip saves in the early stages of the game.
Skipper, Ken Charlery finally set Posh on the way, with a 71st minute goal, when he wriggled his way through a crowded goalmouth. Good fortune then shone on Posh, as a Lee Williams cross ended up in the back of the net, shortly after Charlery's opening goal. However, there was no luck or good fortune with Posh's third goal, Liburd Henry scoring with a strike from substitute David Morrison's quality cross. Dean Trott and Posh centre-back Gary Breen then had a scuffle and were fortunate when referee Kelvin Morton only showed the pair yellow cards, as the incident was worthy of reds, based on the official`s performance though, yellow

Continued...

cards were not a surprise. The referee did at least give Posh a late penalty for handball, after refusing one just as clear in the first half. Charlery won the race to convert the first spot-kick Posh had won this season and made the 4-0 score line look emphatic.
Posh: Scott Cooksey, Kevin Ashley, Tony Spearing, Marcus Ebdon, Gary Breen, Simon Clark, Sean Farrell (sub David Morrison), Brian McGorry, Lee Williams, Ken Charlery, Liburd Henry.
Unused subs: Glen Thomas, Mark Tyler.
Attendance: 8,739

Unfortunately, they were knocked out in the Second Round by Cambridge United, again at home, losing 2-0 to a Cambridge side with plenty of Posh connections. They were managed by Gary Johnson, who later became manager at London Road and their team included future Posh players Jon Sheffield, Marc Joseph, Billy Manuel, Micah Hyde and Steve Butler.

Season **1995/96** saw Posh progress to the Fourth Round by beating Exeter City 1-0 away in the First Round, Bognor Regis Town 4-0 at home in the next round, with Sean Farrell scoring a hat-trick and Wrexham 1-0 at home in the Third Round. Huddersfield Town were the Fourth Round opposition and they ended Posh`s FA Cup hopes for that season, with a 2-0 win at the Alfred McAlpine Stadium.

1996/97 saw Posh require a replay to get past non-league Cheltenham Town in the First Round. After a 0-0 draw at London Road, the replay also ended 0-0 at the end of 90 minutes, but four goals in extra-time saw Posh win 3-1. They also needed a replay to beat another non-league club, Enfield in the Second Round, the first game ended 1-1 at Enfield`s Southbury Road ground, but Posh won the replay 4-1. Plymouth Argyle were beaten 1-0 at Home Park, thanks to a Ken Charlery goal, in the Third Round. The Fourth Round opponents were Wrexham at London Road, Posh twice took the lead, only for Wrexham to pull level and then former Posh player and future Posh coach, Kevin 'Rooster' Russell scored twice to give Wrexham a 4-2 win.

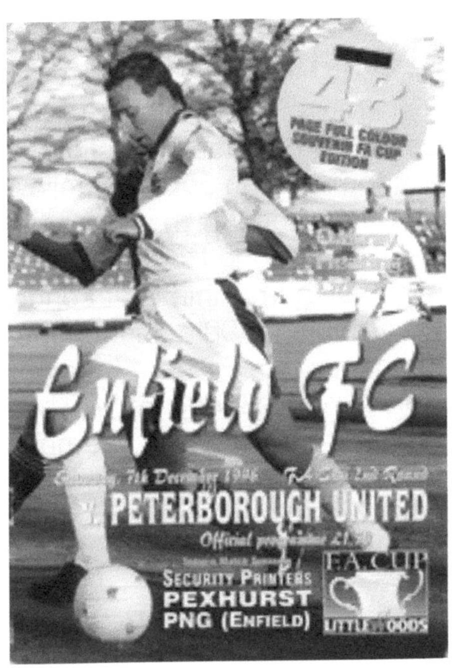

The following season, **1997/98**, Posh made it to the Third Round again, beating Swansea City 4-1 away in the First Round, with Steve Castle scoring twice and Dagenham & Redbridge 3-2 at home in the Second Round, this time with Jimmy Quinn scoring a brace, but they failed to overcome Walsall in the Third Round, losing 2-0 at London Road, a defeat which denied Posh a Fourth Round tie away at Manchester United.

Wrexham dumped Posh out of the cup 1-0 in the First Round in **1998/99,** scoring in the 89th minute at the Racecourse Ground, with Kevin Russell again in The Dragons side, as he had been two seasons before, when they had also knocked Posh out of the cup, also in the Wrexham side was Ian Rush.

The decade ended with another First Round exit for Posh, in **1999/2000**. After a 1-1 draw with Brighton & Hove Albion at London Road, with Andy Clarke scoring for Posh, they lost the replay 3-0 at The Withdean Stadium.

8. The 2000s

The new millennium saw Posh beat Mansfield Town 4-0 in a First Round replay at London Road in **2000/01**, following a 1-1 draw at Field Mill, against a Stags side which included former Posh player Lee Williams. The Second Round also went to a replay, as the first match against Oldham Athletic at London Road ended 1-1, with Jason Lee grabbing a 90th minute equaliser, but Posh won the replay 1-0, thanks to a Richard Forsyth goal, earning themselves a trip to Stamford Bridge in the Third Round. But the reigning FA Cup holders, Chelsea with international stars, including Marcel Desailly, Gus Poyet, Jimmy Floyd Hasselbaink, Dennis Wise, Gianfranco Zola and John Terry in their starting line-up, proved too much for Posh and they went down 5-0.

Match Report

v Chelsea, Stamford Bridge, 3rd Round, 6th January 2001.

Chelsea 5 Posh 0

Up against last season's FA Cup winners and Premiership side, Chelsea at Stamford Bridge, Posh were to say the least up against it in this 3rd Round cup tie. Manager Barry Fry fielded an attacking side, but sadly the forwards saw very little of the ball and it was the Posh defence who had to work hard.

Chelsea started the game briskly, with Mark Tyler diverting a Dennis Wise shot wide before watching Jimmy Floyd Hasselbaink hit a post. But with Andy Edwards and Adam Drury stopping many Chelsea attacks it took until the 37th minute for Chelsea to break the deadlock, Gus Poyet put Gianfranco Zola through towards goal and he chipped the ball into the net from an acute angle. Just before half time, a through ball from David Oldfield gave Andy Clarke a chance to score, but his finishing effort was weak and Posh were immediately punished, as Hasselbaink made it 2-0.

In the second half, David Farrell shot wide from a Howard Forinton pass and a Clarke dribble in the penalty area was wasted by a pointless cutback. Then Chelsea scored three goals in a 12-minute spell, Eidur Gudjohnsen poked home Chelsea's third goal after a smart passing move and Poyet headed home the fourth from an Albert Ferrer cross, it was Poyet again in the 84th minute who sent in a stinging drive, which Tyler couldn't hold and Zola latched onto the ball to score Chelsea's fifth goal.

Whilst all Chelsea's goals had been scored by internationals, Posh fielded many youngsters with both full-backs, Matthew Gill and Gareth Jelleyman, performing well and the work-rate and attitude of strikers Leon McKenzie and Francis Green was commendable.

Posh: Mark Tyler, Adam Drury, Andy Edwards, David Farrell, Leon McKenzie (sub Howard Forinton), David Oldfield, Andy Clarke, Matthew Gill, Francis Green (sub Tony Shields), Gareth Jelleyman (sub Dean Hooper), Richard Forsyth.

Unused subs: Dan Connor, Simon Rea.

Attendance: 31,912

2001/02 saw Posh beat Bedford Town in the First Round, but they needed a replay to do so. After a 0-0 draw away from home, they won the replay at London Road 2-1. The Second Round saw AFC Bournemouth beaten 1-0 at London Road and then Darlington were beaten 2-0 in a Third Round replay, following a 2-2 draw away from home, in which Posh came back from 2-0 down.

Match Report

v Darlington, Feethams, 3rd Round, 15th January 2002.

Darlington 2 Posh 2

Despite being 2-0 down against a mid-table Third Division side, with little over 20 minutes left to play, Posh managed a remarkable comeback which could result in a money-spinning match with Premiership side Newcastle United.

The first chance of the game fell to Danny Mellanby on 3 minutes, when he shot straight at Tyler from the edge of the penalty area, then Barry Conlon did the same soon after, before Mark Ford directed a header from a Wainwright cross close to an upright. A long-range back-header from Ciaran Toner, from a Bullard free-kick, which had Darlington goalkeeper Andy Collett back-pedalling frantically, was the nearest Posh came to scoring in the first half. On 40 minutes Simon Rea was judged to have fouled Danny Mellanby but Posh keeper Mark

Continued...

Tyler brilliantly blocked Brian Atkinson's spot-kick and then kept out Neil Wainwright's follow-up shot only for the referee to order a retake. This time up stepped Conlon to hit the ball so high it not only cleared Tyler's crossbar, but sailed out of the stadium. Two minutes later Tyler was beaten by a Wainwright shot from the edge of the penalty area.
At half-time Dean Hooper and Andy Clarke replaced Marc Joseph and Ciaran Toner and with Leon McKenzie being pushed out to the right-wing, David Farrell moved over to the left flank. There was an immediate improvement as Neale Fenn curled a shot narrowly wide from 20 yards and Clarke went round Collett, but shot from a tight angle rather than cross to better placed team-mates. Then Collett's enormous clearance on the hour was missed by Rea and Conlon beat Andy Edwards to the ball, finishing with a left-foot flick. On 67 minutes Posh pulled a goal back, when Farrell scored from just inside the penalty area. Retribution for the harshly-awarded first-half penalty to Darlington came eight minutes from time, McKenzie was tripped by David Brightwell as he charged through on goal, with Jimmy Bullard smashing home the penalty to force a replay.

Posh: Mark Tyler, Marc Joseph (sub Dean Hooper), Simon Rea, Andy Edwards, David Farrell, David Oldfield, Tom Williams, Jimmy Bullard, Leon McKenzie, Neale Fenn (sub Jon Cullen), Ciaran Toner (sub Andy Clarke).

Unused subs: Dan Connor, Howard Forinton.

Attendance: 6,832

The ‘prize’ in the Fourth Round was a home tie against Newcastle United of the Premier League. Newcastle were managed by Sir Bobby Robson and had England legend Alan Shearer in their starting line-up. Posh put up a brave battle, coming from 2-0 down to level things up at 2-2, before two late goals gave Newcastle a 4-2 win.

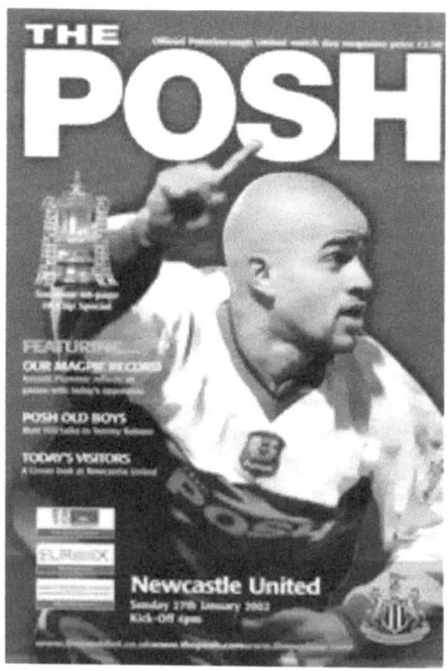

Match Report

v Newcastle Utd, London Road, 4th Round, 27th January 2002.

Posh 2 Newcastle United 4

Two-nil down at half-time on a wet, gloomy Sunday afternoon, Posh staged a fantastic, but doomed, comeback against their Premiership opponents in this cup classic.

In the opening minutes Newcastle looked lively and Alan Shearer scuffed a shot wide of goal on 3 minutes, when Andy Edwards failed to clear. Posh made a swift response, as Leon McKenzie had an effort cleared off the line by Sylvain Distin. Mark Tyler was called into action on 15 minutes, tipping a fierce Olivier Bernard drive round the post. From the resulting corner O'Brien turned on to a Distin header to knock the ball past Tyler. That should have settled the visitors, but they struggled to match the hard-working, effective Posh midfield. A golden chance for Posh to level the scores came on 19 minutes, when McKenzie turned Distin 25 yards out, but his low drive scraped the outside of the far post. Tom Williams saw his stinging effort go narrowly wide of the goal, as Newcastle were beginning to be rattled. Bullard then shaved a post with a whipped free-kick. Just as Posh were starting to inject fear into their opponents and just two minutes before the break, Jamie McClen, playing in his first game for more than two years, scored his first goal for the club with a cool finish.

Within four minutes of the restart, Marc Joseph pelted down the right and delivered a cross to the far post, O'Brien was under no pressure when he headed past his own keeper to make it 2-1. On 69 minutes, David Farrell cut in from the touchline and sent a 20-yard shot past the outstretched right hand of Shay Given to level the scores. Neale Fenn was released by Farrell with 13 minutes to go and one-on-one with Given, his effort was on target, but Given saved it with his left hand. Andy Clarke then went close with a chip, before an Alan Shearer header from Nolberto Solano's free-kick bounced on to the arm of Leon McKenzie. The contact was hardly deliberate, but the referee pointed to the spot and Shearer struck an emphatic penalty past Mark Tyler. A minute later, Aaron Hughes met a cross from Wayne Quinn to make it 4-2.

Posh: Mark Tyler, Marc Joseph, Simon Rea (sub Dean Hooper), Andy Edwards, David Farrell, Andy Clarke, Tom Williams, Jimmy Bullard, Leon McKenzie, Neale Fenn (sub Howard Forinton), Richard Forsyth (sub David Oldfield).

Unused subs: Dan Connor, Jon Cullen.

Attendance: 14,175

Posh went out in the First Round in **2002/03**, losing 3-2 to Rochdale at Spotland, with one of the Rochdale goals scored by Clive Platt, who joined Posh on a free transfer the following season.

Faring better in **2003/04**, Posh progressed to the Third Round, after beating Hereford United 2-0 at London Road in the First Round and Grimsby Town 3-2, also at London Road, in the Second Round. They met Coventry City at Highfield Road in the Third Round, but went out, losing 2-1, having had Sagi Burton sent-off.

In **2004/05**, they went as far as the Fourth Round. Tranmere Rovers were beaten 2-1 at London Road in the First Round, before another home tie in the Second Round saw Posh beat Bath City 2-0. They were drawn away in the Third Round at MK Dons, where they won 2-0. Nottingham Forest were the Fourth Round opponents and Posh went out, losing 1-0 at the City Ground.

2005/06 was another bad season in the FA Cup for Posh, they were drawn at home to Burton Albion, who were then a non-league club, but the game ended goalless and Burton, managed by Nigel Clough went on to win the replay 1-0.

Match Report

v Burton Albion, Pirelli Stadium, 1st Round Replay, 16th November 2005.

Burton Albion 1 Posh 0

This defeat by Conference side Burton Albion was Posh's fifth defeat as a Football League side to non-league opposition. Despite playing well for the first 45 minutes, Posh hardly won any challenges or loose balls in the second half and were embarrassingly dumped out of the FA Cup.

Posh's best chance in the first half came when Danny Crow pounced on a loose ball and after running 30 yards, passed to the unmarked Adam Newton, whose shot was pushed round the post by Burton keeper Saul Deeney. Further chances for Posh came in the first half, with Jamie Day going close with a header from a Dean Holden cross and Holden later picked out Newton for another header, which was easily saved. Lee Thorpe then saw his low strike from the edge of the penalty area turned away by Deeney, as Posh controlled the game.

Continued...

Although Posh keeper Mark Tyler had nothing to do in the first half, it was different story in the second half, as Posh got caught out on numerous occasions and a cup shock looked on the cards. And the shock came in the 74th minute, when Shaun Harrad lifted a close-range shot into the roof of the net, after a hopeful pass went over Posh defender Chris Plummer's head. The expected late Posh onslaught on Burton's goal didn't materialise, though in the 90th minute Jamie Day sent in a drive which was well held by home keeper Saul Deeney. So out went Posh and the chance of a lucrative cup run was gone for another season.

Posh: Mark Tyler, Dean Holden, Paul Carden, Mark Arber, Peter Gain, Adam Newton (sub Ryan Semple), Sean St Ledger, Chris Plummer, Jamie Day, Danny Crow (sub Calum Willock), Lee Thorpe (sub Trevor Benjamin).

Unused subs: Jamie Hand, Sagi Burton.

Attendance: 2,511

Posh beat Rotherham United 3-0 at home in the First Round, in **2006/07**. Then new Posh Chairman, Darragh MacAnthony paid for 28 coaches to take Posh fans to Merseyside for the Second Round tie against Tranmere Rovers, where despite going a goal down, a Danny Crow brace gave Keith Alexander`s side a 2-1 win. The Third Round tie against Plymouth Argyle at London Road ended 1-1, with another missile throwing incident, this time a plastic bottle, which was thrown at the Argyle players as they celebrated their goal in front of the London Road End. No action was taken against Posh and Plymouth`s goal scorer Hasney Aljofree apologised for his actions, his manager Ian Holloway said "the way my players celebrated in front of the Peterborough fans was disrespectful and if I`d been a fan behind that goal, I`d have thrown a bottle myself". The Pilgrims won the replay at Home Park 2-1, with Peterborough-born David Norris scoring the winning goal.

Season **2007/08** saw a 4-1 home win over Wrexham in the First Round, with Craig Mackail-Smith scoring a hat-trick, then a 5-0 away victory over Staines Town in the Second Round, with Mackail-Smith this time scoring four and a 3-1 win over Colchester United at Layer Road, in the Third Round, before Posh bowed out 3-0 at the hands of West Bromwich Albion in the Fourth Round at London Road.

AFC Hornchurch were beaten 1-0 in the First Round of the **2008/09** competition. Tranmere Rovers were the Second Round opposition and after a 0-0 draw at home, Posh won the replay 2-1, with Craig Mackail-Smith scoring the winning goal in extra-time. Then, for the second successive season, it was West Bromwich Albion who put Posh out of the cup. Posh held The Baggies to a 1-1 draw at The Hawthorns, but lost the replay 2-0.

Match Report

v West Bromwich Albion, The Hawthorns, 3rd Round, 3rd January 2009.

West Bromwich Albion 1 Posh 1

West Brom fielded nine of the players who had played in their last Premier League game, yet it was the Posh players who shone, especially in the first half.

Posh almost went ahead in the 24th minute, when Craig Mackail-Smith curled a shot, which Scott Carson in the West Brom goal, finger-tipped onto the woodwork. In another move involving the 'holy trinity', Aaron McLean volleyed straight at Carson, before Chris Whelpdale tested the West Brom keeper from the edge of the penalty-area. Apart from Gaby Zakuani giving Posh keeper Joe Lewis an anxious moment, when his diving-header went just past his own post, West Brom didn't look like scoring and Chris Brunt frustrated the home crowd with shots from distance which went high into the stand behind the Posh goal.

Continued...

West Brom did improve after the interval and Lewis did well at close-range to deny both Luke Moore and Jonathan Greening, before central defender Jonas Olsson headed the home side in front from a Brunt corner. Despite this setback Posh continued to attack, with George Boyd testing Carson from distance, before sending over a delightful cross which Mackail-Smith missed, with the goal at his mercy. Boyd then scored, but referee Kevin Friend disallowed the goal for offside. But Posh weren't to be denied an equaliser, as in the 87th minute McLean sent in a low cross, which Mackail-Smith got to and prodded the ball over the line. Still there was time for more goal-mouth action, as McLean fired wide from the edge of the area and Lewis had to dive full-length to keep out Marek Cech.

Posh: Joe Lewis, Russell Martin, Craig Morgan, Charlie Lee, Aaron McLean (sub Sergio Torres), George Boyd, Dean Keates, Craig Mackail-Smith, Paul Coutts, Gaby Zakuani, Chris Whelpdale (sub Shaun Batt).

Unused subs: James McKeown, Chris Westwood, Dominic Green, Danny Andrew, Danny Blanchett.

Attendance: 18,659

Craig Mackail-Smith`s 12 goals, make him Posh`s joint-second highest scorer in the FA Cup, with Billy Hails.

Posh`s league status meant they came into the **2009/10** competition at the Third Round stage and they were drawn against Tottenham Hotspur. But Posh were no match for the Premier League side and lost 4-0 at White Hart Lane.

Match Report

v Tottenham Hotspur, White Hart Lane, 3rd Round, 2 January 2010.

Tottenham Hotspur 4 Posh 0

Spurs boss, Harry Redknapp fielded a strong side at White Hart Lane, quashing any rumours of key players being saved for the club's quest for a Champions League spot and his team of 11 internationals quickly set about dominating the game, with Posh's lone striker Craig Mackail-Smith looking a very isolated figure. Jermaine Defoe hit the bar from only five yards out, while Tom Huddlestone saw a long-range shot saved by Posh keeper Joe Lewis. A wonderful move from Spurs ended with a back-flick from Defoe setting Niko Kranjcar free in the area, only for Lewis to pull off an outstanding save. But the Croatian was not to be denied for long, breaking free from midfield after being set up by Luka Modric and letting fly with a low shot past Lewis' despairing dive.

Posh never looked likely to get back into the game and any hopes were all but ended when Kranjcar bagged his second after the break, when the midfielder latched on to Gareth Bale's pull-back. Craig Mackail-Smith did see a powerful shot brilliantly saved by Heurelho Gomes, but Tottenham responded by quickly going on the attack to make it 3-0, when another cross from Bale was turned in by Defoe, his 16th goal of the season. Substitute and former Posh loanee, Danny Rose was impressive after coming on in the second half and when he was fouled inside the box late on, Robbie Keane wrapped things up from the penalty-spot.

Posh: Joe Lewis, Tom Williams (sub Tommy Rowe), Craig Morgan, Ryan Bennett, Scott Griffiths, Charlie Lee (sub Dominic Green), Paul Coutts, Lee Frecklington (sub Shaun Batt), Chris Whelpdale, George Boyd, Craig Mackail-Smith.

Unused Subs: James McKeown, Toumani Diagouraga, Romone McCrae, Ben Wright

Attendance: 35,862

9. The 2010s.

Season **2010/11** saw Posh beat Stockport County in the First Round, after a 1-1 draw, they won the replay 4-1 at London Road. Then, in the Second Round, Bury were defeated 2-1 at Gigg Lane. In the Third Round, Posh went out to Fulham of the Premier League, losing 6-2 at Craven Cottage. The Cottagers had Posh legend Simon Davies in their side.

Match Report

v Fulham, Craven Cottage, 3rd Round, 8th January 2011

Fulham 6 Posh 2

In what turned out to be manager Gary Johnson's last game in charge, Fulham showed the gulf in class between the Premier League and League One.

With George Boyd out through injury, Posh almost went ahead in the first five minutes, with David Stockdale forced into saving from Arron Davies, following a corner and then from a drive from Craig Mackail-Smith. Fulham's Simon Davies should have put them ahead, against his former club, when he slashed horribly at a Damien Duff cross. Lee Tomlin blasted narrowly over from 20 yards, after a lightning break before Posh conceded in the 32nd minute, when Chris Baird's far-post cross was nodded home from point-blank range by Kamara. Duff saw a low drive deflected wide, before missing a great chance to make it 2-0, after racing clear and clipping just past the post, but the winger was the creator of the second, on the stroke of half-time, his cross cleared to Dickson Etuhu, who blasted home, via a deflection.

Both sides made a change at the break, Fulham withdrawing Davies for Zoltan Gera and Peterborough, Chris Whelpdale for Nathaniel Mendez-Laing. Posh repeated their flying start in the second half, with Mackail-Smith sending an angled-drive wide and John Pantsil forced to clear acrobatically, after Stockdale made a hash of a corner. Posh responded to the onslaught by handing a debut to Obika, in place of Davies, in the 55th minute, but they were dead and buried four minutes later, Danny Murphy's slide-rule pass broke a non-existent offside-trap and Kamara raced clear, before slotting the ball into the far corner.

Murphy almost put Duff clean through, before the latter produced an inch-perfect cross for Gera to head across Lewis and into the net for Fulham's fourth. Agard came on for Adam Clayton in Posh's final change, 20 minutes from time. Two minutes later, Tomlin scored, arguably the goal of the game, the winger racing in from the right-hand side and blasting a low shot into the far corner. But there was more misery to come for Posh and more joy for Kamara, when the striker side-footed home Greening's cutback from the left, to complete his hat-trick. Posh captain Grant McCann sent Stockdale the wrong way in the 86th minute, but Greening made it 6-2, when he side footed home a minute from time.

Posh: Joe Lewis, Mark Little, Kelvin Langmead, Gaby Zakuani, Grant McCann, Craig Mackail-Smith, Tommy Rowe, Chris Whelpdale (sub Nathaniel Mendez-Laing), Arron Davies (sub Jonathan Obika), Lee Tomlin, Adam Clayton (sub Kieran Agard).

Unused subs: James Wesolowski, Ryan Bennett, Steve Collis, Nana Ofori-Twumasi.

Attendance: 15,936

Being back in the Championship once again, meant Posh`s **2011/12** campaign started in the Third Round, where they were drawn against Sunderland, managed by Martin O`Neill, but they went straight out of the competition, losing 2-0 at London Road.

2012/13 saw Posh fall at the first hurdle again, beaten 3-0 at home by Norwich City, whose side included former Posh players Russell Martin and Ryan Bennett, in the Third Round.

Then in **2013/14** it was back to playing in the First Round for Posh, where they beat Exeter City 2-0 at home. The Second Round saw Tranmere Rovers beaten 5-0 at London Road, with Britt Assombalonga scoring a hat-trick, but the Third Round proved to be an embarrassment for Posh when non-league Kidderminster Harriers held them to a 0-0 draw, only to go on and win the replay 3-2 at London Road, with Michael Gash, who had once been in the youth set-up at Posh as a teenager, on the scoresheet for The Harriers.

Match Report

v Kidderminster Harriers, London Road, 3rd Round Replay,
14th January 2014.
Posh 2 Kidderminster Harriers 3

The Posh served up an embarrassing display in this replay at London Road and were dumped out of the FA Cup by non-league Kidderminster.

Posh had led 1-0 at half-time, after a Danny Kearns' cross, which beat Kidderminster 'keeper Daniel Lewis, hit the far post and the ball was bundled over the line by Tommy Rowe. But even before the goal Kidderminster should have been ahead, they had sliced through the Posh defence, but luckily Amari Morgan-Smith sent his shot straight at Bobby Olejnik.

After the break Posh crumbled, a sweeping move and cross from Danny Jackman saw Michael Gash head the ball home on 49 minutes and three minutes later they were in front, after Joe Lolley's pace was too much for the Posh defence, and Jack Byrne's shot somehow beat Olejnik.

Britt Assombalonga equalised from the penalty-spot, after a fine pass from substitute Danny Swanson unlocked the visiting defence 20 minutes from time, resulting in Lee Vaughan illegally and unnecessarily bringing down Assombalonga in the penalty area. But any thoughts of a fourth round tie at Sunderland were dispelled within two minutes, as Kidderminster won a corner, it was partially cleared and Lolley was given all the time he needed to smash the ball home from 25 yards.

Even when 3-2 down Posh passed the ball backwards and sideways and showed no urgency. Too many Posh players hid, shirked tackles and lacked the skills to trouble the spirited and committed Kidderminster team.

There was no creativity, no spark or vision and as a result Kidderminster saw the game out frighteningly easily. They packed their defence and invited Posh to cross the ball, something they did appallingly. Substitute Grant McCann did swing in a couple of excellent corners, but no-one was brave enough to attack them. Kidderminster remained disciplined, won every tackle that mattered and rarely looked like conceding. Even with four minutes of added time Posh did little and as a result meekly accepted their defeat.

Posh: Bobby Olejnik, Mark Little, Shaun Brisley, Michael Bostwick, Nathaniel Knight-Percival, Danny Kearns (sub Grant McCann), Jack Payne, Jermaine Anderson (sub Danny Swanson), Tommy Rowe (sub Joe Newell), Shaun Jeffers, Britt Assombalonga.

Unused subs: Joe Day, Kgosi Ntlhe, Hogan Ephraim, Charlie Coulson.

Attendance: 3,483

Carlisle United were beaten 2-1 at home in the First Round in **2014/15**, before Posh went out of the competition to Colchester United, losing 1-0 away from home in the Second Round, the only goal of the game was scored by George Moncur, who later briefly spent time on loan at Posh. The winning goal came in the 90th minute, after an Aaron McLean penalty had been saved by Colchester goalkeeper Sam Walker just three minutes earlier.

In **2015/16**, Posh progressed through the first three rounds without conceding a goal, beating Burton Albion 3-0 away in the First Round, then Luton Town, who were managed by John Still and had Posh legends Mark Tyler and Craig Mackail-Smith in their team, 2-0 at home in the Second Round and Preston North End were then beaten 2-0 at London Road in the Third Round. Premier League side, West Bromwich Albion were the Fourth Round opponents and Posh earned themselves a replay at London Road after holding The Baggies to a 2-2 draw at The Hawthorns. The replay went to penalties, after a 1-1 draw, but Posh lost 4-3 in the penalty shoot-out.

Match Report

v West Bromwich Albion, The Hawthorns,4th Round, 30th January 2016.

West Bromwich Albion 2 Posh 2

Posh fought back twice to earn an FA Cup replay, drawing 2-2 after an exciting finale. West Brom began brightly and created two good chances in the first 2 minutes. First James McClean put a low cross straight into the path of Rickie Lambert, but he tried to take a touch and ran the ball out of play. Then McClean almost picked out former Posh loanee Saido Berahino with a cut-back pass, but it went behind the incoming striker. Posh did though fall behind after 14 minutes, when Harry Beautyman gave the ball away, allowing Lambert to lead a West Brom break, Lambert held play up before laying the ball off to Berahino, who beat Ben Alnwick with a 25-yard shot. Posh presented West Brom with two more chances either side of the half-hour mark, first when Michael Smith let Lambert catch him in possession and then, Ricardo Santos gave the ball away to James McClean, with Ben Alnwick doing well on both occasions to stop the home side taking a bigger lead.

Posh cut out the silly mistakes after the break, but West Brom should have increased their lead when Craig Gardner blasted a Salomon Rondon cut-back over. Posh began making inroads and home goalkeeper Boaz Myhill had to get down to smother Smith's low shot on 72 minutes. Just when it looked like Berahino's goal would be all that was needed to settle the game, three goals in eight minutes meant Posh got another chance to beat the Premier League side. On 79 minutes, West Brom were punished when a long ball forward caused Sebastien Pocognoli and Myhill to hesitate and Shaquile Coulthirst scored from the right-side of the penalty box.

With Posh having being level for just 5 minutes, Berahino restored Albion's lead when Posh failed to clear Craig Dawson's cross and the ball found its way to Berahino who finished clinically. But with four minutes left, Jon Taylor found the bottom corner of the net with a shot from the edge of the area to level the scores.

Posh: Ben Alnwick, Michael Smith, Jack Baldwin, Michael Bostwick, Lawrie Wilson (sub Jon Taylor), Erhun Oztumer (sub Marcus Maddison), Ricardo Almeida Santos, Harry Beautyman (sub Martin Samuelsen), Lee Angol, Chris Forrester, Shaquille Coulthirst.

Unused Subs: Andrew Fox, Dion-Curtis Henry, Leonardo da Silva Lopes, Souleymane Coulibaly.

Attendance: 22,517

Match Report

v West Bromwich Albion, London Road, 4th Round Replay, 10th February 2016.

Posh 1 West Bromwich Albion 1 (AET) (West Brom won 4-3 on penalties)

Posh must have felt aggrieved at losing this game. Led by man-of-the-match, West Ham loanee Martin Samuelsen, Posh looked equal to the Premier League side and almost opened the scoring when a Harry Beautyman effort was blocked by James Chester, a former Posh loanee. Posh took the lead when Jon Taylor latched on to a ball by Lee Angol, ran into the area and shot across goal to make it 1-0. Late in the first half, after a lengthy spell of pressure from Posh, West Brom finally found their feet and defender Chester somehow missed the target from a few yards out, following a corner.

In the second half West Brom upped their performance and Fletcher scored when he smashed home from a James McClean cross. After the equaliser it looked as if West Brom would go on to win and in extra-time they had the better of the play.

However, Michael Bostwick and Gaby Zakuani, were astounding in the Posh defence blocking numerous attempts on goal. Saido Berahino should have won it for West Brom in the final seconds of extra-time, but he headed Gardner's free-kick wide before the game went to penalties.

Martin Samuelsen had a spot-kick saved in the shoot-out, but his miss was cancelled out when Fletcher shot wide from his penalty. West Brom led 4-3 in the shoot-out when Posh striker Lee Angol had his spot-kick saved by Ben Foster, to take West Brom through to the 5th Round.

Posh: Ben Alnwick, Andrew Fox, Gaby Zakuani, Jack Baldwin, Michael Bostwick, Martin Samuelsen, Harry Beautyman (sub Marcus Maddison), Chris Forrester, Jon Taylor (sub Erhun Oztumer), Shaquille Coulthirst (sub Souleymane Coulibaly), Lee Angol

Unused Subs: Kgosi Nthle, Harry Toffolo, Dion-Curtis Henry, Leonardo da Silva Lopes.

Attendance: 10,632

2016/17 saw Chesham United beaten 2-1 in the First Round at London Road and Notts County beaten 2-0 in a Second Round replay, following a 2-2 draw at Meadow Lane, after Posh had conceded a two-goal lead, following the controversial sending-off of Lee Angol. The Third Round gave Posh a glamour tie at Stamford Bridge against Chelsea, who sat at the top of the Premier League and although Posh battled hard, they were not disgraced, despite the 4-1 score line in favour of Chelsea, who went all the way to the final that season, losing to Arsenal at Wembley.

Match Report

v Chelsea, Stamford Bridge, 3rd Round, 8th January 2017.

Chelsea 4 Posh 1

Chelsea, top of the Premier League, fielded a weakened starting line-up, but the gulf in class between the two sides was immense. Despite this, on 6 minutes Marcus Maddison delivered a superb cross for Lee Angol six yards from goal, but unfortunately Angol's poke at goal lacked force and precision and Asmir Begovic was able to save easily. After that chance Chelsea dominated and on 18 minutes Pedro scored, after Chris Forrester and Luke McGee had blocked shots from Cesc Fabregas and Nathaniel Chalobah. Pedro then missed an easy chance, striking the bar from just 6 yards, before Batshuayi, a £33million striker, scored to make it 2-0, after Branoslav Ivanovic and Ruben Loftus-Cheek had set him up.
Chelsea should have scored a third goal straight after the interval, as Loftus-Cheek ran through. but he side-footed wide of the goal. Willian made no mistake though on 52 minutes, picking his spot from the edge of the area. A double substitution by Grant McCann had a positive effect, with Paul Taylor proving a handful for the Chelsea defence. Then a pass from Forrester and some Angol trickery, resulted in John Terry clumsily dumping the forward on the floor, which led to an early bath for the former England captain. Three minutes later Tom Nichols scored from a Michael Smith right-wing cross. Any thoughts of a comeback were soon dashed when Pedro claimed his second goal of the game in the 76th minute with an accurate side-foot from 22 yards.

Posh: Luke McGee, Michael Smith, Andrew Hughes, (sub Jerome Binnom-Williams), Michael Bostwick, Ryan Tafazolli, Chris Forrester, Gwion Edwards (sub Martin Samuelsen), Leonardo da Silva Lopes, Marcus Maddison (sub Paul Taylor), Lee Angol, Tom Nichols.
Unused subs: Dominic Ball, Callum Chettle, Brad Inman, Mark Tyler.

Attendance: 41,003

Posh`s FA Cup journey in **2017/18** began with a 1-1 draw at home to Tranmere Rovers in the First Round, before a 5-0 win for Posh in the replay at Prenton Park, with Danny Lloyd scoring a hat-trick. Another non-league club, Woking held Posh to a 1-1 draw in the Second Round, with Joe Ward, who signed for Posh later in the season, scoring the Woking goal, Posh won the replay 5-2 at London Road. In the Third Round, Posh travelled to Villa Park where they came from a goal down to beat Aston Villa 3-1 to earn a place in the Fourth Round. Although Aston Villa were not quite the 'giants' they once were, it was still a significant scalp for Posh against a big team from the division above.

Match Report

v Aston Villa, Villa Park, 3rd Round, 6th January 2018.

Aston Villa 1 Posh 3

Villa must have regretted fielding a weakened team, making 10 changes to the team that played in their last league game, as the Posh came from behind to win 3-1.

Villa started brightly, with Andre Green forcing Posh keeper Jonathan Bond into a fine one-handed save from 20 yards in the opening minutes and they took the lead after eight minutes when Anthony Grant failed to clear, allowing Keinan Davis to score from eight yards. After the goal Posh settled down and were the better side with Villa keeper Jed Steer called into action at full stretch, from both Marcus Maddison and Leo Da Silva Lopes, before using his feet to deny Jack Marriott twice. Liam Shephard almost equalised after 28 minutes, with a looping header that struck the crossbar and Danny Lloyd shot wide from the rebound.

Posh kept up the pressure after the interval, though it was Villa who almost scored, but Jonathan Bond made a smart save, dashing from his line to block a Callum O'Hare shot after 70 minutes. Posh equalised on 76 minutes, after a Forrester run into the area was followed by a cross to Lloyd at the far post, who hit the ball back across goal for Marriott to head home from close range. Then a Maddison corner found Ryan Tafazolli, who headed the ball into the roof of the net. Bond made a couple of good saves before Posh sealed victory with a fast break out of defence, started by Anthony Grant and finished by Marriott from a perfect Maddison cross.

Posh: Jonathan Bond, Liam Shephard, Andrew Hughes, Steven Taylor, Ryan Tafazolli, Anthony Grant, Chris Forrester, Leonardo Da Silva Lopes (sub Junior Morias), Danny Lloyd, Marcus Maddison, Jack Marriott.

Unused subs: Conor O'Malley, Jermaine Anderson, Alex Penny, Michael Doughty, Idris Kanu, Jack Baldwin.

Attendance: 21,677

They were drawn at home to Leicester City, who had been Premier League champions just 18 months earlier, in the Fourth Round, but The Foxes proved too strong for Posh and won 5-1, which was Posh`s biggest ever home defeat in the FA Cup.

Match Report

v Leicester City, London Road, 4th Round, 27th January 2018.

Posh 1 Leicester 5

Despite fielding a weakened team, Premier League side Leicester City thrashed Posh 5-1 in front of a bumper, London Road crowd.

Posh were 1-0 down after just 7 minutes, when Liam Shephard's throw-in to Anthony Grant was intercepted resulting in Fousseni Diabete scoring and just five minutes later it was 2-0 after Chris Forrester's misplaced pass led to Kelechi Iheanacho scoring from the edge of the penalty area. Outclassed, Posh were always second-best and on 29 minutes Iheanacho volleyed a third goal following a left-wing cross. Posh played much better in the first 15

Continued...

minutes of the second half, with Marcus Maddison, Chris Forrester and Jack Marriott getting more involved and making the Leicester City defence work seriously for the first time in the match. A Maddison corner on 57 minutes, led to Posh reducing the arrears to 3-1, with Andrew Hughes scoring from 10 yards, following a Stephen Taylor knock-down. Sadly, Posh faded away and Wilfred Ndidi, Marc Albrighton and Ben Chilwell all tested Posh goalkeeper Jonathan Bond, before Leicester scored twice in the last three minutes through Diabate and Ndidi to make the final score 5-1.

Posh: Jonathan Bond, Liam Shephard, Andrew Hughes, Steven Taylor, Ryan Tafazolli, Anthony Grant, Chris Forrester, Leo Da Silva Lopes (sub Junior Morias), Marcus Maddison (sub Andrea Borg), Danny Lloyd (sub Idris Kanu), Jack Marriott.

Unused subs: Conor O'Malley, Alex Penny, Jack Baldwin, Michael Doughty.

Attendance: 13,193

Danny Lloyd scored a hat-trick against Tranmere Rovers at Prenton Park.

So, to complete Posh`s FA Cup story to date, **2018/19** began with an away tie away at non-league Bromley, a side Posh had never met before in a competitive fixture, where they came from a goal down to win 3-1. The Second Round gave them a home tie against Bradford City, a team they had met many times before, but never in the FA Cup, they were leading 2-0 with six minutes to go and seemingly cruising through to the Third Round, but a late collapse saw The Bantams pull the game back to 2-2, which meant a replay at Valley Parade. The replay ended in a 4-4 draw, with Ivan Toney scoring a hat-trick. Posh eventually won the tie 3-2 on penalties, with goalkeeper Conor O`Malley saving three of Bradford`s spot-kicks.

Ivan Toney Posh`s hat-trick hero
at Valley Parade, Bradford.

The Third Round paired them with Middlesbrough at The Riverside Stadium. Posh were level at 0-0 at half-time, but Boro scored five second-half goals, to win 5-0 and so end Posh`s cup campaign for another season.

Next season maybe, just maybe…

10. Facts & Figures

Overall Record:

P	W	D	L	F	A
284	147	61	76	565	380

First Match:

Date: 5th October 1935

Round: First Qualifying Round

Opponents: Rushden Town

Venue: London Road

Attendance: 4,254

Record Win:

Score: Peterborough United 9 v Rushden Town 1

Date: 6th October 1945

Round: Second Qualifying Round

Venue: Hayden Road, Rushden

Attendance: Unknown

Record Defeat:

Score: Peterborough United 1 v Northampton Town 8

Date: 23rd December 1946

Round: Second Round Replay

Venue: Highfield Road, Coventry

Attendance: 3,164

Highest Home Attendances:

Attendance	Date	Opponents
30,096	20th February 1965	Swansea Town
30,056	30th January 1965	Arsenal
28,266	28th January 1961	Aston Villa
28,174	27th January 1962	Sheffield Utd
28,000	26th January 1974	Leeds Utd

Lowest Home Attendances:

Attendance	Date	Opponents
*0	4th December 1992	Kingstonian
2,312	15th November 2010	Stockport County
2,427	17th October 1936	Wolverton Town
2,563	21st October 1937	Kettering Town
2,778	20th November 1985	Bishop Stortford

* Match played behind closed doors following a FA Disciplinary Committee decision.

Highest Away Attendances:

Attendance	Date	Opponents
64,531	1st February 1961	Aston Villa
63,635	6th March 1965	Chelsea
56,352	24th January 1976	Manchester Utd
51,144	30th January 1960	Sheffield Wednesday
48,735	26th January 1957	Huddersfield Town

Lowest Away Attendances: (Where attendance known)

Attendance	Date	Opponents
1,981	16th November 1985	Bishop's Stortford
2,001	6th November 2010	Stockport County
2,119	14th November 1936	Biggleswade Town
2,460	1st December 2007	Staines Town
2,511	16th November 2005	Burton Albion

Victories, as a non-league club, over League clubs:

Opponents	Division	Date
Torquay Utd	Third (South)	22nd November 1952
Aldershot	Third (South)	12th December 1953
Ipswich Town	Third (South)	19th November 1955
Bradford Park Avenue	Third (North)	8th December 1956
Lincoln City	Second	9th January 1957
Shrewsbury Town	Third	14th November 1959
Walsall	Fourth	5th December 1959
Ipswich Town	Second	9th January 1960

Defeats, as a League club, to non-league clubs:

Opponents	Date
Wigan Athletic (Away)	12th December 1970
Northwich Victoria (Away)	14th December 1976
Dagenham (Away)	8th December 1984
Sutton Utd (Home)	5th December 1987
Burton Albion (Away)	16th November 2005
Kidderminster Harriers (Home)	14th January 2014

Club most drawn against:

Club: Kettering Town

No of times: 10

Season	Round	Home / Away
1936/37	First Qualifying	Away
1937/38	Second Qualifying	Away
1938/39	First Qualifying	Home
1945/46	Second Qualifying	Away
1946/47	Third Qualifying	Home
1947/48	Third Qualifying	Away
1948/49	Third Qualifying	Home
1949/50	Second Qualifying	Away
1950/51	Second Qualifying	Away
1958/59	First Round	Home

Closest to Final:

Closest to final: 6th Round (Quarter-Finals)

Season: 1964/65

Round	Opponents	Score
First	Salisbury	5-1
Second	Queen`s Park Rangers	3-3
Second Replay	Queen`s Park Rangers	2-1
Third	Chesterfield	3-0
Fourth	Arsenal	2-1
Fifth	Swansea Town	0-0
Fifth Replay	Swansea Town	2-0
Sixth	Chelsea	1-5
Semi-final		
Final		

Number of times beaten in first game:

12

Season	Opponents	Score
1935/36	Rushden Town	3-0
1954/55	Boston Utd	2-1
1968/69	Bristol Rovers	3-1
1978/79	Southend Utd	3-2
1979/80	Bournemouth	2-1
1983/84	Oxford Utd	2-0
1986/87	Northampton Town	3-0
1998/99	Wrexham	1-0
2002/03	Rochdale	3-2
2009/10	Tottenham Hotspur	4-0
2011/12	Sunderland	2-0
2012/13	Norwich City	3-0

* Not including replays

Most games in one campaign:

No of games: 9

Season: 1946/47

Round	Opponents	Score
First Qualifying	Wellingborough Town	6-0
Second Qualifying	Westwood Works	3-0
Third Qualifying	Kettering Town	4-1
Fourth Qualifying	Hitchin Town	4-1
First Round	Yeovil Town	2-2
First Round Replay	Yeovil Town	1-0
Second Round	Northampton Town	1-1
Second Round Replay	Northampton Town	1-1
Second Round 2nd Replay	Northampton Town	1-8

First Hat-trick

Scorer: Charlie MacCartney

Date: 20th October 1938

Round: Second Qualifying Round Replay

Opponents: Rushden Town

Venue: London Road

Result: Peterborough United 3 v Rushden Town 1

Other players who have scored hat-tricks:

Player	Date	Opposition
Tommy Rudkin	16th November 1946	Hitchin Town
Andy Donaldson	9th January 1957	Lincoln City
Jimmy Longworth	2nd November 1957	Wolverton Town & BR
Dennis Emery	1st November 1958	Walthamstow Avenue
George Hudson	13th November 1961	Colchester United
Derek Dougan	14th November 1964	Salisbury
Derek Dougan	9th January 1965	Chesterfield
Tommy Watson	28th January 1967	Bedford Town
John Fairbrother	11th December 1967	Falmouth Town
Dave Longhurst	19th November 1988	Gillingham
Sean Farrell	2nd December 1996	Bognor Regis Town
Craig Mackail-Smith	10th November 2007	Wrexham
Britt Assombalonga	7th December 2013	Tranmere Rovers
Danny Lloyd	15th November 2017	Tranmere Rovers
Ivan Toney	11th December 2018	Bradford City

Top Goal Scorers:

	Player	Goals
1.	Dennis Emery	31
2.	Billy Hails / Craig Mackail-Smith	12
4.	Jim Hall / Freddie Martin	11

Most goals in a single game:

No of goals: 6

Player: Ken Laxton

Date: 6th October 1945

Round: Second Qualifying

Opponents: Rushden Town

Venue: Hayden Road, Rushden

Result: Rushden Town 1 v Peterborough United 9

Other players who have scored more than 3 goals in a game:

No of goals	Player	Date	Opposition
4	Fred Warnes	5th October 1946	Wellingborough Town
4	Craig Mackail-Smith	1st December 2007	Staines Town

*Tony Philliskirk scored 5 goals against Kingstonian on 25th November 1992 in a 9-1 win. The match was declared void and ordered to be replayed.

Most goals in one campaign:

No of goals: 9

Scorer: Charlie MacCartney

Season: 1938/39

Goals	Opponents	Round
1	Kettering Town	First Qualifying Round
2	Rushden Town	Second Qualifying Round
3	Rushden Town	Second Qualifying Round Replay
2	Spalding United	Third Qualifying Round
1	St Neots Town & District	Fourth Qualifying Round

Most Appearances:

	Player	Apps
1.	Tommy Robson	43 + 2 Sub
2.	Norman Rigby	41
3.	Billy Hails	35
4.	Dennis Emery Chris Turner Mark Tyler	33

Record for scoring in consecutive games:

No of games: 10

Player: Dennis Emery

Date from: 6th November 1954

Date to: 9th January 1957

Date	Round	Goals	Opponents	Score
6th Nov 1954	Fourth Qualifying	1	Boston Utd	1-2
5th Nov 1955	Fourth Qualifying	1	Ilkeston Town	3-1
19th Nov 1955	First Round	2	Ipswich Town	3-1
10th Dec 1955	Second Round	1	Swindon Town	1-1
15th Dec 1955	Second Round Replay	1	Swindon Town	1-2
3rd Nov 1956	Fourth Qualifying	2	Corby Town	5-1
17th Nov 1956	First Round	2	Yeovil Town	3-1
8th Dec 1956	Second Round	1	Bradford Park Avenue	3-0
5th Jan 1957	Third Round	2	Lincoln City	2-2
9th Jan 1957	Third Round Replay	1	Lincoln City	5-4

First player to be sent off for Posh in the FA Cup:

Player: Jim Hall

Date: 22nd November 1971

Round: First Round Replay

Opponents: Redditch United

Venue: London Road

Result: Peterborough United 6 v Redditch United 0

Most sent off Posh player in the FA Cup:

No of times: 2

Player: Sagi Burton

3rd January 2004 v Coventry City 3rd Rd (Away) Lost 2-1

13th November 2004 v Tranmere Rovers 1st Rd (Home) Won 2-1

Other Posh players sent off:

Player	Date	Opposition
Gerry McElhinney	12th December 1990	Wycombe Wanderers (Away)
Craig Morgan	26th January 2008	West Bromwich Albion (Home)
Jack Baldwin	7th November 2015	Burton Albion (Away)
Lee Angol	4th December 2016	Notts County (Away)

Teams Played Against:

Team	P	W	D	L	F	A
Kettering Town	13	7	3	3	30	19
Tranmere Rovers	9	7	2	0	22	4
Colchester Utd	7	4	2	1	17	9
Northampton Town	7	3	2	2	12	14
Hereford Utd	6	3	2	1	10	5
Torquay Utd	6	3	1	2	12	8
Chesterfield	5	3	2	0	10	5
Rushden Town	5	3	1	1	20	11
Gillingham	5	2	2	1	8	9
Plymouth Argyle	5	2	1	2	7	6
West Bromwich Albion	5	0	3	2	4	9
Enfield	4	3	1	0	10	2
Bedford Town	4	3	1	0	10	4

Team	P	W	D	L	F	A
Notts County	4	3	1	0	8	2
Bishop Stortford	4	2	2	0	10	6
Corby Town	4	2	1	1	10	5
Wrexham	4	2	0	2	7	6
Newcastle Utd	4	1	1	2	4	7
Brighton & Hove Albion	4	0	2	2	3	7
Wellingborough Town	3	3	0	0	14	2
Symington`s Recreation	3	3	0	0	12	2
Spalding Utd	3	2	1	0	8	4
Wycombe Wanderers	3	2	1	0	6	2
Yeovil Town	3	2	1	0	6	3
Ipswich Town	3	2	0	1	6	5
Walsall	3	2	0	1	5	5
Weymouth	3	1	2	0	6	3
Aston Villa	3	1	1	1	5	4
Kidderminster Harriers	3	1	1	1	4	4
Burton Albion	3	1	1	1	3	1
Nottingham Forest	3	1	1	1	1	1
Tottenham Hotspur	3	0	2	1	2	6
Fulham	3	0	1	2	2	7
Middlesbrough	3	0	1	2	1	8
Bristol Rovers	3	0	0	3	2	8
Chelsea	3	0	0	3	2	14
Wolverton Town	2	2	0	0	10	0
Falmouth Town	2	2	0	0	9	3
Westwood Works	2	2	0	0	8	0
Desborough Town	2	2	0	0	7	2
Hitchin Town	2	2	0	0	7	2
Rotherham Utd	2	2	0	0	4	0
Bath City	2	2	0	0	3	0
Exeter City	2	2	0	0	3	0
Barnet	2	2	0	0	3	1
Carlisle United	2	2	0	0	3	1

Team	P	W	D	L	F	A
Redditch Utd	2	1	1	0	7	1
Lincoln City	2	1	1	0	7	6
Woking	2	1	1	0	6	3
Mansfield Town	2	1	1	0	5	1
Stockport County	2	1	1	0	5	2
Queen`s Park Rangers	2	1	1	0	5	4
Darlington	2	1	1	0	4	2
Cheltenham Town	2	1	1	0	3	1
Swansea Town *	2	1	1	0	2	0
Hayes	2	1	1	0	2	1
Kingstonian	2	1	1	0	2	1
Oldham Athletic	2	1	1	0	2	1
Shrewsbury Town	2	1	0	1	6	6
Southend Utd	2	1	0	1	5	4
Swansea City *	2	1	0	1	5	4
Cardiff City	2	1	0	1	3	4
AFC Bournemouth	2	1	0	1	2	2
Cambridge Utd	2	1	0	1	2	2
Portsmouth	2	1	0	1	2	2
Luton Town	2	1	0	1	2	3
Leeds Utd	2	1	0	1	2	4
Bradford City	2	0	2	0	6	6
Brentford	2	0	1	1	2	3
Watford	2	0	1	1	2	3
Reading	2	0	1	1	0	1
Huddersfield Town	2	0	0	2	1	5
Sunderland	2	0	0	2	1	9
Derby County	2	0	0	2	0	3
Harlow Town	1	1	0	0	7	0
Bury Town	1	1	0	0	7	1
Staines Town	1	1	0	0	5	0
Salisbury	1	1	0	0	5	1
Doncaster Rovers	1	1	0	0	5	2

Team	P	W	D	L	F	A
Bognor Regis Town	1	1	0	0	4	0
Coventry Sporting	1	1	0	0	4	0
Margate	1	1	0	0	4	0
Dover	1	1	0	0	4	1
Grays Athletic	1	1	0	0	4	1
Winsford Utd	1	1	0	0	4	1
Headington Utd **	1	1	0	0	4	2
Bradford Park Avenue	1	1	0	0	3	0
Charlton Athletic	1	1	0	0	3	0
Halifax Town	1	1	0	0	3	0
Walthamstow Av	1	1	0	0	3	0
Bromley	1	1	0	0	3	1
Ilkeston Town	1	1	0	0	3	1
Ransome & Marles	1	1	0	0	3	1
Wimbledon	1	1	0	0	3	1
Dagenham & Redbridge	1	1	0	0	3	2
Grimsby Town	1	1	0	0	3	2
MK Dons	1	1	0	0	2	0
Preston North End	1	1	0	0	2	0
Aldershot	1	1	0	0	2	1
Arsenal	1	1	0	0	2	1
Biggleswade Town	1	1	0	0	2	1
Bury	1	1	0	0	2	1
Chesham Utd	1	1	0	0	2	1
Stafford Rangers	1	1	0	0	2	1
AFC Hornchurch	1	1	0	0	1	0
St Neots Town & District	1	1	0	0	1	0
Rochdale	1	0	0	1	2	3
Boston Utd	1	0	0	1	1	2
Coventry City	1	0	0	1	1	2
Port Vale	1	0	0	1	1	2
Vauxhall Motors	1	0	0	1	1	2
Wigan Athletic	1	0	0	1	1	2

Team	P	W	D	L	F	A
Manchester Utd	1	0	0	1	1	3
Sheffield Utd	1	0	0	1	1	3
Sutton Utd	1	0	0	1	1	3
Leicester City	1	0	0	1	1	5
Bristol City	1	0	0	1	0	1
Dagenham	1	0	0	1	0	1
Manchester City	1	0	0	1	0	1
Oxford Utd **	1	0	0	1	0	2
Sheffield Wednesday	1	0	0	1	0	2
Dartford	1	0	0	1	0	3
Norwich City	1	0	0	1	0	3
Northwich Victoria	1	0	0	1	0	4

NB. Games decided by penalty shoot-outs count as a draw, whether won or lost on penalties.
** Headington United renamed Oxford United in 1960.
* Swansea Town renamed Swansea City in 1969.

11. Manager`s Records

Manager	Period	P	W	D	L	F	A
Jock Porter	1934/36	1	0	0	1	0	3
Fred Taylor	1936/37	5	4	0	1	11	6
Bert Poulter	1937/38	3	1	1	1	7	3
Sam Haden	1938/48	21	13	4	4	59	35
Jack Blood	1948/50	8	6	0	2	22	7
Bob Gurney	1950/52	5	1	2	2	7	6
George Swindin	1954/58	14	7	3	4	38	22
Jimmy Hagan	1958/61	22	13	5	4	54	32
Johnny Anderson	1962/63	2	2	0	0	4	0
Jack Fairbrother	1952/54 1962/64	15	8	3	4	31	21
Gordon Clark	1964/67	14	9	2	3	36	25
Norman Rigby	1967/69	4	2	0	2	10	6
Jim Iley	1968/72	10	6	1	3	23	12
John Barnwell	1977/78	5	2	2	1	6	5
Billy Hails	1978/79	1	0	0	1	2	3
Peter Morris	1979/82	10	6	1	3	15	8
Martin Wilkinson	1982/83	4	2	1	1	9	8
John Wile	1983/86	10	5	2	3	12	9
Lil Fuccillo	1986/87	1	0	0	1	0	3
Noel Cantwell	1972/77 1986/88	25	14	5	6	46	31
Mick Jones	1988/89	4	1	2	1	6	6
Mark Lawrenson	1989/90	3	1	1	1	3	4
Dave Booth	1990/91	5	2	2	1	7	5
Chris Turner	1991/92 1993/94	8	2	4	2	13	7
John Still	1994/95	2	1	0	1	4	2
Mick Halsall	1995/96	4	3	0	1	6	2
Barry Fry	1996/05	31	15	7	9	49	40
Mark Wright	2005/06	2	0	1	1	0	1
Keith Alexander	2006/07	3	2	1	0	6	2
Tommy Taylor	2007	1	0	0	1	1	2
Mark Cooper	2009/10	1	0	0	1	0	4
Gary Johnson	2010/11	4	2	1	1	9	9

Manager	Period	P	W	D	L	F	A
Darren Ferguson	2007/09 2012/15	17	8	3	6	27	19
Graham Westley	2015/16	5	3	2	0	10	3
Grant McCann	2016/18	10	5	3	2	23	17
Steve Evans	2018/19	4	1	2	1	9	12

Most games as manager:

Manager	Period	Games	Wins	Win Ratio
Barry Fry	1996/2005	31	15	48%
Noel Cantwell	1972/1977 1986/1988	25	14	56%
Jimmy Hagan	1958/1961	22	13	59%
Sam Haden	1938/1948	21	13	62%
Darren Ferguson	2007/2009 2012/2015	17	8	47%

Best manager win ratios:

Manager	Period	Games	Wins	Win Ratio
Johnny Anderson	1962/63	2	2	100%
Fred Taylor	1936/37	5	4	80%
Jack Blood	1948/50	8	6	75%
Mick Halsall	1995/96	4	3	75%
Keith Alexander	2006/07	3	2	66%

12. Results

Season	Round	Home or Away	Opponents	Score	Posh Goal Scorers
1935/36	1st Qualifying	Home	Rushden Town	0-3	
1936/37	1st Qualifying	Away	Kettering Town	2-0	Ted Chiverton, Jack Wilson
	2nd Qualifying	Home	Wolverton Town	3-0	Jack Briggs (2), Jack Wilson
	3rd Qualifying	Home	Rushden Town	4-2	Harry Roberts (2), Jack Briggs, Jack Wilson
	4th Qualifying	Away	Biggleswade Town	2-1	Jack Briggs, Jack Wilson
	1st Round	Away	Dartford	0-3	
1937/38	1st Qualifying	Away	Wellingborough Town	5-0	Tommy Atkin (2), Cyril Boulton (2), Sam Rowbotham
	2nd Qualifying	Away	Kettering Town	2-2	George Bowater, Cyril Boulton
	2nd Qualifying Replay	Home	Kettering Town	0-1	
1938/39	1st Qualifying	Home	Kettering Town	2-1	Charlie MacCartney, Eric Bott
	2nd Qualifying	Away	Rushden Town	4-4	Horace Fielding, Charlie MacCartney (2), Eric Bott
	2nd Qualifying Replay	Home	Rushden Town	3-1	Charlie MacCartney (3)
	3rd Qualifying	Away	Spalding Utd	3-2	Charlie MacCartney (2), George Bowater
	4th Qualifying	Home	St Neots Town	1-0	Charlie MacCartney
	1st Round	Away	Bristol Rovers	1-4	Horace Fielding
1945/46	2nd Qualifying	Away	Rushden Town	9-1	Jack Polhill, Ken Laxton (6), Hubert Tasker, Rodgers
	3rd Qualifying	Away	Kettering Town	1-2	Fred Fairchild
1946/47	1st Qualifying	Home	Wellingborough Town	6-0	Fred Warnes (4), Alan Scobie, John Padgett
	2nd Qualifying	Home	Westwood Works	3-0	Tommy Rickards, Fred Warnes, Alan Scobie
	3rd Qualifying	Home	Kettering Town	4-1	Adam Mitchell, Alan Scobie, Tommy Rudkin, Nat Brooksbank
	4th Qualifying	Home	Hitchin Town	4-1	Adam Mitchell, Tommy Rudkin (3)
	1st Round	Away	Yeovil Town	2-2	Ken Bayliss, Tommy Rudkin
	1st Round Replay	Home	Yeovil Town	1-0	Tommy Rudkin
	2nd Round	Home	Northampton Town	1-1	Arnold Bramham
	2nd Round Replay	Away	Northampton Town	1-1	John Padgett
	2nd Round 2nd Replay	Neutral	Northampton Town	1-8	Nat Brooksbank

1947/48	1st Qualifying	Home	Westwood Works	5-0	Jack Ranshaw (2), Nat Brooksbank (2), Ron Jones
	2nd Qualifying	Away	Desborough Town	2-1	Colin Rawson, Arnold Bramham
	3rd Qualifying	Away	Kettering Town	4-3	Nat Brooksbank, Tommy Rickards (2), Frank Squires,
	4th Qualifying	Away	Vauxhall Motors	1-2	Frank Squires
1948/49	1st Qualifying	Home	Symington`s Recreation	4-0	Tommy Rickards, Johnny McGuinn, Billy Guest, Harold Huxford
	2nd Qualifying	Away	Wellingborough Town	3-2	Tommy Rickards, Glyn Vaughan, Harold Huxford
	3rd Qualifying	Home	Kettering Town	2-1	Billy Guest, Joe Sanderson
	4th Qualifying	Home	Ransome & Marles	3-1	Tommy Rickards, Nat Brooksbank, Joe Sanderson
	1st Round	Home	Torquay Utd	0-1	
1949/50	1st Qualifying	Home	Desborough Town	5-1	Roy Houghton, Ted Widdowfield (2), Freddie Martin (2)
	2nd Qualifying	Away	Kettering Town	5-0	Jim Fallon, Ted Widdowfield (2), Arnold Robinson (2)
	3rd Qualifying	Away	Corby Town	0-1	
1950/51	1st Qualifying	Home	Symington`s Recreation	3-0	Freddie Martin, Martin Jennings, Paddy Foley
	2nd Qualifying	Away	Kettering Town	2-2	Frank Bee, Arnold Robinson
	2nd Qualifying Replay	Home	Kettering Town	1-2	Paddy Foley
1951/52	4th Qualifying	Home	Hereford Utd	1-1	Freddie Martin
	4th Qualifying Replay	Away	Hereford Utd	0-1	
1952/53	1st Qualifying	Away	Symington`s Recreation	5-2	John Anderson, Paddy Sloan, Andy Donaldson, Freddie Martin, George Hair
	2nd Qualifying	Away	Spalding Utd	2-2	Norman Rigby, Andy Donaldson
	2nd Qualifying Replay	Home	Spalding Utd	3-0	Norman Rigby, Dougald Campbell, Paddy Sloan
	3rd Qualifying	Away	Corby Town	0-0	
	3rd Qualifying Replay	Home	Corby Town	5-3	Freddie Martin, George Hair, Norman Rigby, Andy Donaldson, Dougald Campbell
	4th Qualifying	Home	Bedford Town	2-1	Andy Donaldson, Freddie Martin
	1st Round	Home	Torquay Utd	2-1	Paddy Sloan, Freddie Martin
	2nd Round	Home	Bristol Rovers	0-1	
1953/54	4th Qualifying	Home	Grays Athletic	4-1	Freddie Marin, Barry Matthews, Own Goals (2)
	1st Round	Away	Hitchin Town	3-1	Dougald Campbell, Doug Taft (2)
	2nd Round	Home	Aldershot	2-1	Freddie Martin, Doug Taft
	3rd Round	Away	Cardiff City	1-3	Freddie Martin
1954/55	4th Qualifying	Home	Boston Utd	1-2	Dennis Emery

1955/56	4th Qualifying	Away	Ilkeston Town	3-1	Billy Hails (2), Dennis Emery
	1st Round	Home	Ipswich Town	3-1	Dennis Emery (2), George Hair
	2nd Round	Away	Swindon Town	1-1	Dennis Emery
	2nd Round Replay	Home	Swindon Town	1-2	Dennis Emery
1956/57	4th Qualifying	Away	Corby Town	5-1	Dennis Emery (2), Bob Gibson (2), Ray Smith
	1st Round	Away	Yeovil Town	3-1	Billy Hails, Dennis Emery (2)
	2nd Round	Home	Bradford Park Avenue	3-0	Billy Hails, Dennis Emery, Andy Donaldson
	3rd Round	Home	Lincoln City	2-2	Dennis Emery (2)
	3rd Round Replay	Away	Lincoln City	5-4	Dennis Emery, Andy Donaldson (3), Ray Smith
	4th Round	Away	Huddersfield Town	1-3	Bernard Shaw
1957/58	4th Qualifying	Home	Wolverton Town & BR	7-0	Dennis Emery, Jimmy Longworth (3), Ray Smith, Own Goals (2)
	1st Round	Home	Torquay Utd	3-3	Dennis Emery, Andy Donaldson (2)
	1st Round Replay	Away	Torquay Utd	0-1	
1958/59	4th Qualifying	Home	Walthamstow Av	3-0	Dennis Emery (3)
	1st Round	Home	Kettering Town	2-2	Dennis Emery, Billy Hails
	1st Round Replay	Away	Kettering Town	3-2	Dennis Emery, Billy Hails, Own Goal
	2nd Round	Home	Headington Utd	4-2	Billy Hails, Dennis Emery (2), Jim Rayner
	3rd Round	Away	Fulham	0-0	
	3rd Round Replay	Home	Fulham	0-1	
1959/60	4th Qualifying	Home	Bury Town	7-1	Billy Hails (2), Jim Rayner, Dennis Emery, Ray Smith (2), Peter McNamee
	1st Round	Home	Shrewsbury Town	4-3	Jim Rayner, Dennis Emery (2), Ray Smith
	2nd Round	Away	Walsall	3-2	Jim Rayner, Ray Smith, Peter McNamee
	3rd Round	Away	Ipswich Town	3-2	Jim Rayner, Dennis Emery (2)
	4th Round	Away	Sheffield Wednesday	0-2	
1960/61	1st Round	Away	Dover	4-1	Dennis Emery (2), Terry Bly, Keith Ripley
	2nd Round	Away	Torquay Utd	3-1	Terry Bly, Peter McNamee (2)
	3rd Round	Away	Portsmouth	2-1	Billy Hails, Keith Ripley
	4th Round	Home	Aston Villa	1-1	Billy Hails
	4th Round Replay	Away	Aston Villa	1-2	Peter McNamee
1961/62	1st Round	Home	Colchester Utd	3-3	Terry Bly, Peter McNamee, George Hudson
	1st Round Replay	Away	Colchester Utd	2-2	Dennis Emery, Terry Bly
	1st Round 2nd Replay	Neutral	Colchester Utd	3-0	George Hudson (3)
	2nd Round	Away	Torquay Utd	4-1	Billy Hails, Terry Bly, George Hudson (2)
	3rd Round	Away	Newcastle Utd	1-0	Terry Bly
	4th Round	Home	Sheffield Utd	1-3	George Hudson
1962/63	1st Round	Away	Notts County	3-0	George Hudson (2), Peter McNamee
	2nd Round	Home	Enfield	1-0	George Hudson
	3rd Round	Away	Derby County	0-2	
1963/64	1st Round	Home	Watford	1-1	Own Goal
	1st Round Replay	Away	Watford	1-2	Roy Senior

1964/65	1st Round	Home	Salisbury	5-1	Vic Crowe, Derek Dougan (3), Peter Deakin
	2nd Round	Away	QPR	3-3	Ron Barnes, Peter McNamee, Peter Deakin
	2nd Round Replay	Home	QPR	2-1	Peter Deakin (2)
	3rd Round	Away	Chesterfield	3-0	Derek Dougan (3)
	4th Round	Home	Arsenal	2-1	Derek Dougan, Peter McNamee
	5th Round	Home	Swansea Town	0-0	
	5th Round Replay	Away	Swansea Town	2-0	Peter Deakin (2)
	6th Round	Away	Chelsea	1-5	Vic Crowe
1965/66	1st Round	Home	Kidderminster Harriers	2-1	Peter Deakin (2)
	2nd Round	Away	Shrewsbury Town	2-3	Peter Deakin, Graham Birks
1966/67	1st Round	Home	Hereford Utd	4-1	John Fairbrother, Johnny Byrne, Ollie Conmy, Own Goal
	2nd Round	Away	Colchester Utd	3-0	Tommy Watson (2), John Fairbrother
	3rd Round	Away	Bedford Town	6-2	Harry Orr, Tommy Watson (3), John Fairbrother, Ollie Conmy
	4th Round	Away	Sunderland	1-7	Tommy Watson
1967/68	1st Round	Home	Falmouth Town	5-2	Johnny Byrne, John Fairbrother (3), Stuart Brace
	2nd Round	Away	Margate	4-0	Ollie Conmy, Peter Deakin, Peter Thompson, Stuart Brace
	3rd Round	Home	Portsmouth	0-1	
1968/69	1st Round	Away	Bristol Rovers	1-3	Bobby Downes
1969/70	1st Round	Away	Falmouth Town	4-1	Peter Price, Tommy Robson, Jim Hall (2)
	2nd Round	Home	Plymouth Argyle	2-0	Peter Price, Ollie Conmy
	3rd Round	Away	Rotherham Utd	1-0	Jim Hall
	4th Round	Away	Gillingham	1-5	Peter Price
1970/71	1st Round	Home	Wimbledon	3-1	Jim Hall, Colin Garwood, Bobby Moss
	2nd Round	Away	Wigan Athletic	1-2	Bobby Moss
1971/72	1st Round	Away	Redditch Utd	1-1	Peter Price
	1st Round Replay	Home	Redditch Utd	6-0	Peter Price, Jim Hall (2), Tommy Robson, Richie Barker (2)
	2nd Round	Home	Enfield	4-0	Peter Price (2), Jim Hall (2)
	3rd Round	Home	Ipswich Town	0-2	
1972/73	1st Round	Home	Northampton Town	1-0	Jim Hall
	2nd Round	Away	Bishop Stortford	2-2	John Cozens, Tommy Robson
	2nd Round Replay	Home	Bishop Stortford	3-1	Tommy Robson, Don Heath, Jim Hall
	3rd Round	Home	Derby County	0-1	
1973/74	1st Round	Away	Colchester Utd	3-2	John Cozens (2), Bert Murray
	2nd Round	Away	Wycombe Wanderers	3-1	John Cozens (2), Jim Hall
	3rd Round	Home	Southend Utd	3-1	John Cozens, Freddie Hill, Tommy Robson
	4th Round	Home	Leeds Utd	1-4	John Cozens

1974/75	1st Round	Home	Weymouth	0-0	
	1st Round Replay	Away	Weymouth	3-3	David Gregory, Chris Turner, David Llewellyn
	1st Round 2nd Replay	Home	Weymouth	3-0	Chris Turner, David Gregory (2)
	2nd Round	Home	Charlton Athletic	3-0	Bert Murray, Jon Nixon, David Gregory
	3rd Round	Home	Tranmere Rovers	1-0	Keith Bradley
	4th Round	Away	Stafford Rangers	2-1	Jon Nixon, David Gregory
	5th Round	Home	Middlesbrough	1-1	Jon Nixon
	5th Round Replay	Away	Middlesbrough	0-2	
1975/76	1st Round	Home	Winsford Utd	4-1	Jon Nixon, John Cozens, David Gregory, Chris Turner
	2nd Round	Away	Coventry Sporting	4-0	Lyndon Hughes, Mick Jones, Jon Nixon, Own Goal
	3rd Round	Away	Nottingham Forest	0-0	
	3rd Round Replay	Home	Nottingham Forest	1-0	Jon Nixon
	4th Round	Away	Manchester Utd	1-3	John Cozens
1976/77	1st Round	Away	Tranmere Rovers	4-0	John Cozens, Ernie Moss, Jack Carmichael, Tommy Robson
	2nd Round	Away	Northwich Victoria	ABND	Jon Nixon
	2nd Round	Away	Northwich Victoria	0-4	
1977/78	1st Round	Away	Barnet	2-1	Alan Slough, Tommy Robson
	2nd Round	Away	Gillingham	1-1	Alan Slough
	2nd Round Replay	Home	Gillingham	2-0	Jack Carmichael, Gary Sargent
	3rd Round	Home	Newcastle Utd	1-1	Gary Sargent
	3rd Round Replay	Away	Newcastle Utd	0-2	
1978/79	1st Round	Away	Southend Utd	2-3	Barry Butlin, Trevor Anderson
1979/80	1st Round	Home	AFC Bournemouth	1-2	Billy Kellock
1980/81	1st Round	Away	Northampton Town	4-1	Tommy Robson (2), Trevor Quow, Trevor Slack
	2nd Round	Away	Barnet	1-0	Tommy Robson
	3rd Round	Home	Chesterfield	1-1	Robbie Cooke
	3rd Round Replay	Away	Chesterfield	2-1	Robbie Cooke (2)
	4th Round	Away	Notts County	1-0	Robbie Cooke
	5th Round	Home	Manchester City	0-1	
1981/82	1st Round	Away	Halifax Town	3-0	Robbie Cooke (2), Dave Syrett
	2nd Round	Home	Walsall	2-1	Robbie Cooke, Phil Chard
	3rd Round	Home	Bristol City	0-1	
1982/83	1st Round	Away	Chesterfield	2-2	Colin Clarke, Micky Gynn
	1st Round Replay	Home	Chesterfield	2-1	Micky Gynn, Colin Clarke
	2nd Round	Home	Doncaster Rovers	5-2	Robbie Cooke (2), Colin Clarke, Trevor Quow, Micky Gynn
	3rd Round	Away	Luton Town	0-3	
1983/84	1st Round	Away	Oxford Utd	0-2	
1984/85	1st Round	Away	Cambridge Utd	2-0	Errington Kelly (2)
	2nd Round	Away	Dagenham	0-1	

1985/86	1st Round	Away	Bishop Stortford	2-2	Gary Worrall, Own Goal
	1st Round Replay	Home	Bishop Stortford	3-1	Francis Cassidy, Jackie Gallagher, Andy Kowalski
	2nd Round	Home	Bath City	1-0	Jackie Gallagher
	3rd Round	Home	Leeds Utd	1-0	Greig Shepherd
	4th Round	Home	Carlisle Utd	1-0	Greig Shepherd
	5th Round	Home	Brighton & Hove Albion	2-2	Greig Shepherd, Errington Kelly
	5th Round Replay	Away	Brighton & Hove Albion	0-1	
1986/87	1st Round	Away	Northampton Town	0-3	
1987/88	1st Round	Home	Cardiff City	2-1	Mick Gooding (2)
	2nd Round	Home	Sutton Utd	1-3	Les Lawrence
1988/89	1st Round	Away	Gillingham	3-3	David Longhurst (3)
	1st Round Replay	Home	Gillingham	1-0	Own Goal
	2nd Round	Home	Brentford	0-0	
	2nd Round Replay	Away	Brentford	2-3	Mick Halsall, Nick Cusack
1989/90	1st Round	Home	Hayes	1-1	Worrell Sterling
	1st Round Replay	Away	Hayes	1-0	Dave Robinson
	2nd Round	Away	Swansea City	1-3	Gary Andrews
1990/91	1st Round	Away	Hereford Utd	1-1	David Riley
	1st Round Replay	Home	Hereford Utd	2-1	Worrell Sterling, David Riley
	2nd Round	Away	Wycombe Wanderers	1-1	Paul Culpin
	2nd Round Replay	Home	Wycombe Wanderers	2-0	Mick Halsall, Paul Culpin
	3rd Round	Away	Port Vale	1-2	Mick Halsall
1991/92	1st Round	Home	Harlow Town	7-0	Gary Cooper (2), David Riley, Worrell Sterling, Mick Halsall, Ken Charlery, Paul Culpin
	2nd Round	Home	Reading	0-0	
	2nd Round Replay	Away	Reading	0-1	
1992/93	1st Round	Away	Kingstonian	1-1	Tony Adcock
	1st Round Replay	Home	*Kingstonian	9-1	Tony Philliskirk (5), Tony Adcock (2), Gary Cooper, Own Goal
	1st Round Replay	Home	**Kingstonian	1-0	Worrell Sterling
	2nd Round	Away	Plymouth Argyle	2-3	Tony Philliskirk, Worrell Sterling
1993/94	3rd Round	Home	Tottenham Hotspur	1-1	Jason Brissett
	3rd Round Replay	Away	Tottenham Hotspur	1-1	Ken Charlery
1994/95	1st Round	Home	Northampton Town	4-0	Ken Charlery (2), Lee Williams, Liburd Henry
	2nd Round	Home	Cambridge Utd	0-2	
1995/96	1st Round	Away	Exeter City	1-0	Neil Le Bihan
	2nd Round	Home	Bognor Regis Town	4-0	Sean Farrell (3), Marcus Ebdon
	3rd Round	Home	Wrexham	1-0	Neil Le Bihan
	4th Round	Away	Huddersfield Town	0-2	

*Match Void
**Played Behind Closed Doors

1996/97	1st Round	Home	Cheltenham Town	0-0	
	1st Round Replay	Away	Cheltenham Town	3-1	Ken Charlery (2), Giuliano Grazioli
	2nd Round	Away	Enfield	1-1	Ken Charlery
	2nd Round Replay	Home	Enfield	4-1	Scott Houghton, Martin Carruthers (2), Ken Charlery,
	3rd Round	Away	Plymouth Argyle	1-0	Ken Charlery
	4th Round	Home	Wrexham	2-4	Ken Charlery, Carl Griffiths
1997/98	1st Round	Away	Swansea City	4-1	Jimmy Quinn, Steve Castle (2), Martin Carruthers
	2nd Round	Home	Dagenham & Redbridge	3-2	Martin Carruthers, Jimmy Quinn (2)
	3rd Round	Home	Walsall	0-2	
1998/99	1st Round	Away	Wrexham	0-1	
1999/00	1st Round	Home	Brighton & Hove Albion	1-1	Andy Clarke
	1st Round Replay	Away	Brighton & Hove Albion	0-3	
2000/01	1st Round	Away	Mansfield Town	1-1	David Farrell
	1st Round Replay	Home	Mansfield Town	4-0	David Oldfield, Andy Edwards, Andy Clarke, Tony Shields
	2nd Round	Home	Oldham Athletic	1-1	Jason Lee
	2nd Round Replay	Away	Oldham Athletic	1-0	Richard Forsyth
	3rd Round	Away	Chelsea	0-5	
2001/02	1st Round	Away	Bedford Town	0-0	
	1st Round Replay	Home	Bedford Town	2-1	Andy Clarke, Neale Fenn
	2nd Round	Home	AFC Bournemouth	1-0	Helgi Danielsson
	3rd Round	Away	Darlington	2-2	David Farrell, Jimmy Bullard
	3rd Round Replay	Home	Darlington	2-0	Leon McKenzie, Andy Clarke
	4th Round	Home	Newcastle Utd	2-4	David Farrell, Own Goal
2002/03	1st Round	Away	Rochdale	2-3	Neale Fenn, Andy Clarke
2003/04	1st Round	Home	Hereford Utd	2-0	Calum Willock, Richard Logan
	2nd Round	Home	Grimsby Town	3-2	Andy Clarke, Steven Thomson, Adam Newton
	3rd Round	Away	Coventry City	1-2	Andy Clarke
2004/05	1st Round	Home	Tranmere Rovers	2-1	Peter Kennedy, Curtis Woodhouse
	2nd Round	Home	Bath City	2-0	Calum Willock (2)
	3rd Round	Away	MK Dons	2-0	Richard Logan, Mark Arber
	4th Round	Away	Nottingham Forest	0-1	
2005/06	1st Round	Home	Burton Albion	0-0	
	1st Round Replay	Away	Burton Albion	0-1	
2006/07	1st Round	Home	Rotherham Utd	3-0	Richard Butcher, Aaron McLean, Danny Crow
	2nd Round	Away	Tranmere Rovers	2-1	Danny Crow (2)
	3rd Round	Home	Plymouth Argyle	1-1	Aaron McLean
	3rd Round Replay	Away	Plymouth Argyle	1-2	Aaron McLean

2007/08	1st Round	Home	Wrexham	4-1	Craig Mackail-Smith (3), Aaron McLean
	2nd Round	Away	Staines Town	5-0	Craig Mackail-Smith (4), Aaron McLean
	3rd Round	Away	Colchester Utd	3-1	Aaron McLean, George Boyd, Charlie Lee
	4th Round	Home	West Bromwich Albion	0-3	
2008/09	1st Round	Away	AFC Hornchurch	1-0	Craig Mackail-Smith
	2nd Round	Home	Tranmere Rovers	0-0	
	2nd Round Replay	Away	Tranmere Rovers	2-1	Aaron McLean, Craig Mackail-Smith
	3rd Round	Away	West Bromwich Albion	1-1	Craig Mackail-Smith
	3rd Round Replay	Home	West Bromwich Albion	0-2	
2009/10	3rd Round	Away	Tottenham Hotspur	0-4	
2010/11	1st Round	Away	Stockport County	1-1	Aaron McLean
	1st Round Replay	Home	Stockport County	4-1	Kelvin Langmead, Craig Mackail-Smith, Lee Tomlin, Aaron McLean
	2nd Round	Away	Bury	2-1	Lee Tomlin, Craig Mackail-Smith
	3rd Round	Away	Fulham	2-6	Lee Tomlin, Grant McCann
2011/12	3rd Round	Home	Sunderland	0-2	
2012/13	3rd Round	Home	Norwich City	0-3	
2013/14	1st Round	Home	Exeter City	2-0	Britt Assombalonga, Nathaniel Mendez-Laing
	2nd Round	Home	Tranmere Rovers	5-0	Britt Assombalonga (3), Shaun Jeffers (2)
	3rd Round	Away	Kidderminster Harriers	0-0	
	3rd Round Replay	Home	Kidderminster Harriers	2-3	Tommy Rowe, Britt Assombalonga
2014/15	1st Round	Home	Carlisle Utd	2-1	Christian Burgess (2)
	2nd Round	Away	Colchester Utd	0-1	
2015/16	1st Round	Away	Burton Albion	3-0	Conor Washington (2), Jermaine Anderson
	2nd Round	Home	Luton Town	2-0	Conor Washington, Marcus Maddison
	3rd Round	Home	Preston North End	2-0	Martin Samuelson, Conor Washington
	4th Round	Away	West Bromwich Albion	2-2	Shaquile Coulthirst, Jon Taylor
	4th Round Replay	Home	West Bromwich Albion	1-1	Jon Taylor
2016/17	1st Round	Home	Chesham Utd	2-1	Shaquile Coulthirst
	2nd Round	Away	Notts County	2-2	Leonardo Da Silva Lopes, Gwion Edwards
	2nd Round Replay	Home	Notts County	2-0	Gwion Edwards, Paul Taylor
	3rd Round	Away	Chelsea	1-4	Tom Nichols

2017/18	1st Round	Home	Tranmere Rovers	1-1	Jack Marriott
	1st Round Replay	Away	Tranmere Rovers	5-0	Danny Lloyd (3), Jack Baldwin, Marcus Maddison
	2nd Round	Away	Woking	1-1	Ryan Tafazolli
	2nd Round Replay	Home	Woking	5-2	Michael Doughty, Jack Marriott (2), Marcus Maddison, Gwion Edwards
	3rd Round	Away	Aston Villa	3-1	Jack Marriott (2), Ryan Tafazolli
	4th Round	Home	Leicester City	1-5	Andrew Hughes
2018/19	1st Round	Away	Bromley	3-1	Matt Godden (2), Joe Ward
	2nd Round	Home	Bradford City	2-2	Ivan Toney, Siriki Dembele
	2nd Round Replay	Away	Bradford City	4-4	Ivan Toney (3), Marcus Maddison
	3rd Round	Away	Middlesbrough	0-5	

13. Player Records

First Name	Surname	Period	Apps	Sub	Un-used Sub	Goals
George	Adams	1966/67 - 1967/68	1	1	3	0
Tony	Adcock	1992/93 - 1993/94	5	0	0	1
Miles	Addison	2015/16	0	0	2	0
Kieran	Agard	2010/11	0	1	0	0
Nicky	Ajose	2012/13	0	1	0	0
Craig	Alcock	2011/12 - 2013/14	3	0	0	0
Ben	Alnwick	2014/15 - 2015/16	7	0	0	0
Harry	Anderson	2015/16	0	0	1	0
Jermaine	Anderson	2013/14 - 2017/18	6	2	5	1
John	Anderson	1952/53 - 1953/54	12	0	0	1
Trevor	Anderson	1978/79	1	0	0	1
Danny	Andrew	2008/09	0	0	1	0
Gary	Andrews	1988/89 - 1989/90	4	0	0	1
Lee	Angol	2015/16 - 2016/17	7	1	0	0
Mark	Arber	2003/04 - 2006/07	11	0	0	1
Kevin	Ashley	1994/95 - 1995/96	4	0	0	0
Britt	Assombalonga	2013/14	4	0	0	5
Mike	Astbury	1985/86	3	0	0	0
Tommy	Atkin	1937/38	3	0	0	2
Jack	Baldwin	2015/16 - 2017/18	5	2	3	1
Dominic	Ball	2016/17	0	0	1	0
Roy	Banham	1958/59 - 1961/62	11	0	0	0
Keith	Bannister	1957/58	1	0	0	0
Fred	Barber	1991/92 - 1993/94	5	0	0	0
Richie	Barker	1971/72	4	0	0	2
Bobby	Barnes	1992/93	0	1	0	0
Ron	Barnes	1964/65 - 1965/66	9	0	0	1
Tyrone	Barnett	2013/14	1	0	1	0
Ray	Barr	1956/57	6	0	0	0
Arthur	Barraclough	1935/36	1	0	0	0
Jim	Barron	1977/78	5	0	0	0
Mike	Basham	1996/97	0	1	0	0
Sebastien	Bassong	2018/19	0	0	2	0

First Name	Surname	Period	Apps	Sub	Un-used	Goals
Shaun	Batt	2008/09 - 2009/10	1	5	0	0
Ken	Bayliss	1946/47	2	0	0	1
Ernest	Beardshaw	1946/47	1	0	0	0
Len	Beaumont	1948/49	1	0	0	0
Harry	Beautyman	2015/16	3	1	1	0
Frank	Bee	1950/51	3	0	0	1
Kenny	Beech	1983/84 - 1984/85	3	0	0	0
Mike	Beesley	1966/67	1	0	0	0
Ian	Benjamin	1982/83 - 1983/84	5	0	0	0
Trevor	Benjamin	2005/06 - 2006/07	1	4	0	0
Ian	Bennett	1992/93	3	0	0	0
Rhys	Bennett	2018/19	3	0	1	0
Ryan	Bennett	2009/10 - 2011/12	5	0	1	0
George	Berry	1990/91	0	0	3	0
David	Bickerstaff	1954/55	1	0	0	0
Jerome	Binnom Williams	2016/17	0	2	2	0
Graham	Birks	1964/65 - 1965/66	8	0	0	1
Charlie	Bisby	1936/37	5	0	0	0
Danny	Blanchett	2007/08 - 2008/09	1	0	5	0
Jack	Blood	1948/49	3	0	0	0
Terry	Bly	1960/61 - 1961/62	11	0	0	6
Mick	Bodley	1996/97 - 1998/99	8	0	0	0
Jonathan	Bond	2017/18	4	0	2	0
Adrian	Boothroyd	1996/97	4	1	0	0
Andrea	Borg	2017/18	0	1	0	0
Michael	Bostwick	2012/13 - 2016/17	15	0	0	0
Eric	Bott	1938/39	3	0	0	2
Andre	Boucaud	2004/05	1	0	2	0
Cyril	Boulton	1937/38	2	0	0	3
George	Bowater	1937/38 - 1938/39	8	0	0	2
George	Boyd	2007/08 - 2012/13	14	0	0	1
Stuart	Brace	1967/68	3	0	0	2
Keith	Bradley	1972/73 - 1975/76	12	1	0	1
Darren	Bradshaw	1992/93 - 1993/94	4	0	0	0
Paul	Bradshaw	1990/91	5	0	0	0
Arnold	Bramham	1946/47 - 1947/48	8	0	0	2
Guy	Branston	2006/07	2	1	0	0
Gary	Breen	1994/95 - 1995/96	6	0	0	0
Kevin	Bremner	1990/91	3	0	0	0
Jack	Briggs	1936/37	5	0	0	4

First Name	Surname	Period	Apps	Sub	Un-used	Goals
Shaun	Brisley	2012/13 - 2013/14	5	0	0	0
Jason	Brissett	1993/94 - 1994/95	2	1	0	1
Eric	Brookes	1971/72 - 1972/73	7	0	0	0
Nat	Brooksbank	1946/47 - 1948/49	11	0	0	6
Drewe	Broughton	1999/2000	0	0	2	0
Bernie	Bryan	1945/46 - 1950/51	24	0	0	0
David	Buchanan	1983/84	0	1	0	0
Jimmy	Bullard	2001/02 - 2002/03	6	0	0	1
Wayne	Bullimore	1997/98	0	1	1	0
Christian	Burgess	2014/15	2	0	0	2
Sagi	Burton	2002/03 - 2005/06	6	0	3	0
Stan	Burton	1947/48	2	0	0	0
Richard	Butcher	2006/07	4	0	0	1
Geoff	Butler	1981/82	3	0	0	0
Steve	Butler	1998/99	1	0	0	0
Barry	Butlin	1977/78 - 1978/79	4	0	0	1
Gary	Butterworth	1987/88 - 1991/92	8	1	1	0
Johnny	Byrne	1965/66 - 1967/68	6	0	0	2
Dougald	Campbell	1952/53 - 1953/54	12	0	0	3
Paul	Carden	2005/06	2	0	0	0
Jack	Carmichael	1971/72 - 1979/80	30	3	0	2
Ashley	Carr	1987/88 - 1988/89	1	1	2	0
Martin	Carruthers	1996/97 - 1997/98	6	0	0	4
Danny	Carter	1995/96 - 1996/97	2	1	0	0
Ian	Carter	1993/94	1	0	0	0
Regan	Carthey	2013/14	0	0	1	0
Sam	Cartwright	2017/18	0	0	1	0
Francis	Cassidy	1984/85 - 1985/86	7	0	2	1
Steve	Castle	1997/98 - 1999/00	4	1	0	2
Derek	Chadwick	1957/58 - 1959/60	14	0	0	0
Aaron	Chapman	2018/19	2	0	2	0
Phil	Chapple	1999/00	1	0	0	0
Phil	Chard	1979/80 -1984/85	9	0	1	1
Kenny	Charlery	1991/92 - 1996/97	11	1	0	10
Kieran	Charnock	2007/08	2	0	0	0
Callum	Chettle	2016/17 - 2017/18	0	0	5	0
Ted	Chiverton	1936/37	5	0	0	1
Derrick	Christie	1986/87	1	0	0	0
Simon	Clark	1994/95 - 1996/97	12	0	0	0
Andy	Clarke	1999/2000 - 2004/05	15	3	1	7
Colin	Clarke	1982/83	4	0	0	2

First Name	Surname	Period	Apps	Sub	Un-used	Goals
Jim	Clarke	1955/56	4	0	0	0
George	Clarke	1937/38	3	0	0	0
Jonson	Clarke-Harris	2012/13	0	0	1	0
Adam	Clayton	2010/11	1	0	0	0
Chris	Cleaver	1996/97 - 1998/99	0	2	1	0
Tony	Cliss	1979/80 - 1982/83	1	2	3	0
Henry	Cockburn	1956/57	6	0	0	0
Bert	Cockroft	1948/49 - 1949/50	8	0	0	0
Ronnie	Codd	1956/57	1	0	0	0
Dave	Collins	1935/36	1	0	0	0
Steve	Collins	1979/80 - 1988/89	15	0	0	0
Steve	Collis	2010/11	0	0	4	0
Walter	Compton	1938/39	1	0	0	0
Tom	Conlon	2013/14	0	1	2	0
Ollie	Conmy	1964/65 - 1971/72	25	0	0	4
Dan	Connor	2000/01 - 2002/03	0	0	12	0
Callum	Cooke	2018/19	0	1	0	0
Robbie	Cooke	1980/81 - 1982/83	13	0	0	10
Scott	Cooksey	1994/95	2	0	0	0
Gary	Cooper	1991/92 - 1992/93	5	0	0	2
George	Cooper	2018/19	1	1	2	0
Ron	Cooper	1959/60 - 1967/68	17	0	0	0
Souleymane	Coulibaly	2015/16	0	2	3	0
Charlie	Coulson	2013/14	0	0	1	0
Shaquile	Coulthirst	2015/16 - 2016/17	4	1	0	3
Paul	Coutts	2008/09 - 2009/10	5	0	0	0
John	Cozens	1972/73 - 1976/77	12	1	0	10
Ian	Crawford	1964/65 - 1968/69	9	0	0	0
Paul	Crichton	1988/89 - 1989/90	5	0	0	0
Phil	Crosby	1989/90 - 1990/91	8	0	0	0
Danny	Crow	2005/06 - 2007/08	6	0	1	3
Vic	Crowe	1964/65 - 1965/66	9	0	0	2
Jon	Cullen	2000/01 - 2001/02	1	2	4	0
Paul	Culpin	1989/90 - 1991/92	4	5	2	3
Jason	Cummings	2018/19	2	2	0	0
Nick	Cusack	1988/89	4	0	0	1
Leonardo	da Silva Lopes	2014/15 - 2017/18	10	0	4	1
Tom	Daley	1959/60	5	0	0	0
Colin	Daniel	2018/19	2	0	0	0
Helgi	Danielsson	2001/02 - 2002/03	2	0	2	1
Micky	Darrell	1971/72	0	1	0	0

First Name	Surname	Period	Apps	Sub	Un-used	Goals
Aaron	Davies	2010/11	3	1	0	0
Jay	Davies	2010/11	0	0	3	0
Simon	Davies	1998/99 - 1999/2000	3	0	0	0
Liam	Davis	2006/07	0	0	1	0
Jamie	Day	2005/06 - 2007/08	6	0	2	0
Joe	Day	2012/13 - 2013/14	0	0	5	0
Miguel	De Souza	1997/98	0	0	1	0
Peter	Deakin	1964/65 - 1967/68	11	0	0	10
Siriki	Dembele	2018/19	3	1	0	1
Tyler	Denton	2018/19	1	0	3	0
Willie	Devlin	1954/55	1	0	0	0
Toumani	Diagouraga	2009/10	0	0	1	0
Edward	Dickens	1938/39	6	0	0	0
Andy	Donaldson	1951/52 - 1957/58	21	0	0	10
Derek	Dougan	1963/64 - 1964/65	10	0	0	7
Michael	Doughty	2017/18	3	0	3	1
Norman	Douglass	1956/57	6	0	0	0
Bobby	Downes	1968/69	1	0	0	1
Johnny	Dowson	1951/52	2	0	0	0
Jeff	Doyle	1986/87	1	0	0	0
Bob	Doyle	1976/77 - 1978/79	8	0	0	0
Mick	Drewery	1969/70 - 1973/74	18	0	0	0
Adam	Drury	1997/98 - 2000/04	9	0	1	0
Willie	Duff	1963/64 - 1965/66	9	0	0	0
John	Duncliffe	1970/71 - 1972/73	6	0	0	0
Steve	Earle	1977/78	1	0	0	0
Marcus	Ebdon	1991/92 - 1996/97	12	3	0	1
Andy	Edwards	1996/97 - 2002/03	21	0	0	1
Gwion	Edwards	2016/17 - 2017/18	6	1	0	3
Callum	Elder	2015/16	2	0	0	0
Frank	Ellmer	1947/48	1	0	0	0
Denis	Emery	1954/55 - 1962/63	33	0	0	31
Hogan	Ephraim	2013/14	1	1	1	0
Matthew	Etherington	1998/99 - 1999/2000	2	1	0	0
Peter	Eustace	1975/76	5	0	0	0
Jack	Fairbrother	1952/53 - 1953/54	12	0	0	0
John	Fairbrother	1965/66 - 1967/68	7	0	0	6
Fred	Fairchild	1945/46	2	0	0	1
Jim	Fallon	1948/49 - 1949/50	8	0	0	1
David	Farrell	1997/98 - 2005/06	21	2	0	3
Sean	Farrell	1994/95 - 1995/96	4	1	0	3

First Name	Surname	Period	Apps	Sub	Un-used	Goals
Des	Farrow	1955/56	4	0	0	0
Neale	Fenn	2001/02 - 2002/03	6	1	0	2
Kane	Ferdinand	2012/13 - 2014/15	1	0	1	0
Bob	Ferguson	1947/48 - 1948/49	9	0	0	0
Horace	Fielding	1938/39	6	0	0	2
Neil	Firm	1982/83	4	0	0	0
Paddy	Foley	1949/50 - 1950/51	4	0	0	2
Mark	Foran	1997/98	1	0	0	0
Howard	Forinton	1999/00 - 2001/02	2	5	3	0
Chris	Forrester	2015/16 - 2017/18	12	2	0	0
Richard	Forsyth	2000/01 - 2002/03	9	0	0	1
Colin	Foster	1979/80	1	0	0	0
Andrew	Fotiadis	2003/04	0	0	1	0
Andrew	Fox	2015/16	1	3	1	0
Reg	Foxall	1937/38	2	0	0	0
Lee	Frecklington	2009/10	1	0	0	0
Neil	Freeman	1981/82	3	0	0	0
Lewis	Freestone	2017/18	0	0	1	0
Daniel	French	1999/2000	0	1	1	0
T	Froggatt	1936/37	5	0	0	0
Lil	Fuccillo	1985/86	7	0	0	0
Andy	Furnell	1993/94 - 1995/96	0	2	0	0
Ben	Futcher	2006/07	3	0	1	0
Wakeley	Gage	1986/87	1	0	0	0
Peter	Gain	2005/06 - 2006/07	2	2	0	0
Jackie	Gallagher	1985/86 - 1986/87	4	2	1	2
Colin	Garwood	1969/70 - 1970/71	3	3	0	1
Sam	Gaughran	2008/09	0	0	3	0
Jimmy	Ghaichem	2006/07	0	0	1	0
Bob	Gibson	1955/56 -1956/57	8	0	0	2
Matthew	Gill	1998/99 - 2003/04	6	1	4	0
Claude	Gnakpa	2007/08	2	1	1	0
Matt	Godden	2018/19	2	2	0	2
Tony	Godden	1989/90	2	0	0	0
Craig	Goldsmith	1988/89	4	0	0	0
Mick	Gooding	1987/88	1	0	0	2
Jaanai	Gordon	2011/12 - 2012/13	0	1	1	0
Barry	Gould	1965/66	1	0	0	0
Milton	Graham	1989/90	2	1	0	0
Anthony	Grant	2017/18	6	0	0	0
Giuliano	Grazioli	1996/97	0	3	0	1

First Name	Surname	Period	Apps	Sub	Un-used	Goals
Dominic	Green	2008/09 - 2009/10	1	2	3	0
Francis	Green	1999/00 - 2001/02	5	0	4	0
Chris	Greenman	1993/94	2	0	0	0
David	Gregory	1974/75 - 1986/87	14	1	0	6
David	Gregory	1995/96	1	0	0	0
Bart	Griemink	1996/97 - 1999/2000	4	0	6	0
Carl	Griffiths	1996/97	1	1	0	1
Scott	Griffiths	2009/10	1	0	0	0
Billy	Guest	1948/49	5	0	0	2
Bryn	Gunn	1986/87 - 1988/89	7	0	0	0
Alan	Guy	1980/81	1	0	0	0
Micky	Gynn	1980/81 - 1982/83	13	0	0	3
Sam	Haden	1938/39	6	0	0	0
Billy	Hails	1955/56 - 1961/62	35	0	0	12
George	Hair	1951/52 - 1955/56	17	0	0	3
George	Hall	1951/52 - 1953/54	7	0	0	0
Jim	Hall	1968/69 - 1974/75	19	1	0	11
Mick	Halsall	1987/88 - 1992/93	20	0	0	4
Jamie	Hand	2005/06	0	0	2	0
Richie	Hanlon	2000/01	0	1	0	0
Len	Hargreaves	1935/36 - 1936/37	5	0	0	0
Jim	Harkin	1948/49	5	0	0	0
David	Harle	1989/90	0	0	1	0
Tom	Harris	1947/48	4	0	0	0
Greg	Heald	1995/96 - 1996/97	8	1	0	0
Don	Heath	1972/73	4	0	0	1
Dion-Curtis	Henry	2014/15 - 2015/16	0	0	7	0
Liburd	Henry	1994/95	2	0	0	1
Dave	Hibbert	2010/11	0	2	0	0
Rodney	Hicks	2006/07	0	0	1	0
Freddie	Hill	1973/74 - 1974/75	10	1	0	1
William	Hilliard	1945/46	2	0	0	0
Peter	Hindley	1976/77 - 1978/79	6	0	0	0
Mark	Hine	1990/91	5	0	0	0
Tom	Hobbs	1945/46	2	0	0	0
Gordon	Hodgson	1980/81 - 1981/2	8	0	0	0
Jack	Hogg	1956/57	4	0	0	0
Dean	Holden	2005/06 - 2006/07	4	0	0	0
Eddie	Holliday	1969/70	1	0	0	0
Jimmy	Holmes	1984/85 - 1985/86	4	0	0	0
Dean	Hooper	1998/99 - 2001/02	7	4	2	0

First Name	Surname	Period	Apps	Sub	Un-used	Goals
Ollie	Hopkins	1961/62 - 1962/63	8	0	0	0
Roy	Horobin	1962/63 - 1963/64	5	0	0	0
Roy	Houghton	1949/50	3	0	0	1
Scott	Houghton	1996/97 - 1997/98	7	0	0	1
Lee	Howarth	1992/93 - 1993/94	3	0	0	0
Rene	Howe	2007/08	0	2	1	0
George	Hudson	1961/62 - 1962/63	9	0	0	10
Andrew	Hughes	2016/17 - 2017/18	10	0	0	1
Jeff	Hughes	2007/08	1	1	0	0
Lyndon	Hughes	1975/76 - 1977/78	7	0	0	1
Shane	Huke	2006/07	3	0	0	0
Harold	Huxford	1948/49	3	0	0	2
Micah	Hyde	2007/08	3	0	0	0
Jim	Iley	1969/70 - 1970/71	5	0	0	0
Mike	Imlach	1983/84	1	0	0	0
Brad	Inman	2016/17	0	1	2	0
Niall	Inman	1996/97	0	1	0	0
Dominic	Iorfa	1992/93 - 1993/94	2	2	1	0
Craig	Ireland	2004/05	1	0	0	0
Brian	Jackson	1962/63	3	0	0	0
Roy	Jacobs	1957/58	2	0	0	0
Shwan	Jalal	2007/08	0	0	2	0
Luke	James	2014/15	0	1	1	0
Derek	Jeffries	1976/77	2	0	0	0
Shaun	Jeffers	2013/14	3	0	1	2
Arthur	Jefferson	1935/36	1	0	0	0
Gareth	Jelleyman	1999/00 - 2004/05	7	2	2	0
Martin	Jennings	1950/51	3	0	0	1
David	Johnson	1984/85 - 1985/86	1	0	2	0
Peter	Johnson	1965/66 - 1966/67	4	0	1	0
Peter	Johnson	1991/92	3	0	0	0
Mick	Jones	1973/74 - 1975/76	7	1	2	1
Paul	Jones	2011/12	0	0	1	0
Ron	Jones	1947/48	1	0	0	1
Marcus	Joseph	2001/02 - 2002/03	6	0	0	0
Christopher	Kanu	2003/04 - 2004/05	2	1	1	0
Idris	Kanu	2017/18	0	3	3	0
Daniel	Kearns	2011/12 - 2013/14	1	1	0	0
Dean	Keates	2007/08 - 2008/09	7	1	1	0
Billy	Kellock	1979/80 - 1981/82	10	0	0	1
Errington	Kelly	1984/85 - 1987/88	8	2	0	3

First Name	Surname	Period	Apps	Sub	Un-used	Goals
Jimmy	Kelly	1954/55	1	0	0	0
Jack	Kendall	1935/36 - 1937/38	9	0	0	0
Peter	Kennedy	2004/05	1	1	0	1
Roy	Killin	1954/55 - 1955/56	5	0	0	0
Gary	Kimble	1991/92	3	0	0	0
John	Kirkham	1965/66 - 1966/67	5	0	0	0
Brian	Klug	1984/85	2	0	0	0
Nathan	Knight-Percival	2012/13 - 2013/14	2	1	1	0
Andy	Kowalski	1985/86	7	0	0	1
Detsi	Kruszynski	1993/94	2	0	0	0
Dickie	Kwiatkowski	1969/70	1	0	0	0
Daniel	Lafferty	2018/19	1	0	0	0
David	Langan	1988/89	1	0	0	0
Kelvin	Langmead	2010/11	4	0	0	1
Dan	Lawlor	2011/12	0	0	1	0
Les	Lawrence	1986/87 - 1987/88	3	0	0	1
Ken	Laxton	1945/46	2	0	0	6
Neil	Le Bihan	1995/96	2	1	1	2
Charlie	Lee	2007/08 - 2010/11	8	1	1	1
Jason	Lee	2000/01 - 2002/03	5	0	0	1
Jeff	Lee	1973/74 - 1977/78	19	0	0	0
Andy	Legg	2003/04 - 2004/05	4	1	1	0
Joe	Lewis	2007/08 - 2011/12	12	0	0	0
Neil	Lewis	1997/98	3	0	0	0
John	Linnell	1967/68	1	0	1	0
Des	Linton	1997/98 - 1998/99	3	1	0	0
Ivor	Linton	1982/83	0	0	1	0
Mark	Little	2010/11 - 2013/14	8	2	0	0
Dave	Llewelyn	1973/74 - 1974/75	4	0	0	1
Danny	Lloyd	2017/18	3	1	2	3
Richard	Logan	2003/04 - 2004/05	4	2	1	2
David	Longhurst	1988/89 - 1989/90	5	1	0	3
Jimmy	Longworth	1956/57 - 1957/58	4	0	0	3
Tony	Lormor	1994/95	1	0	0	0
Josh	Low	2006/07 - 2007/08	2	2	1	0
Jerry	Lowery	1955/56	4	0	0	0
Noel	Luke	1987/88 - 1992/93	18	2	0	0
Frank	Macauley	1936/37	1	0	0	0
Charlie	MacCartney	1938/39	6	0	0	9
Gary	MacDonald	2001/02	1	0	0	0
Jack	Machin	1950/51	3	0	0	0

First Name	Surname	Period	Apps	Sub	Un-used	Goals
Craig	Mackail-Smith	2007/08 - 2010/11	13	1	0	12
Marcus	Maddison	2015/16 - 2018/19	11	4	2	4
Carl	Madrick	1988/89	0	0	4	0
Billy	Manuel	1995/96	1	1	0	0
Jack	Marriott	2017/18	6	0	0	5
Henry	Marsden	1935/36	1	0	0	0
Liam	Marshall	2013/14	0	0	2	0
Freddie	Martin	1949/50 - 1954/55	20	0	0	11
Russell	Martin	2008/09	4	0	0	0
Gary	Martindale	1995/96	4	0	0	0
John	Mason	1966/67 - 1967/68	3	0	0	0
Steve	Massey	1981/82	1	1	1	0
Barry	Matthews	1953/54	3	0	0	1
Mike	Maynard	1967/68	1	0	0	0
Tom	McAnearney	1965/66	1	0	0	0
Jimmy	McCabe	1954/55	1	0	0	0
Grant	McCann	2010/11 - 2014/15	5	2	2	1
	McClelland	1945/46	1	0	0	0
Romone	McCrae	2009/10	0	0	1	0
Charles	McDonagh	1937/38 - 1938/39	9	0	0	0
David	McDonald	1993/94	2	0	0	0
Gerry	McElhinney	1988/89 - 1990/91	12	0	0	0
Kenneth	McEvoy	2014/15	0	0	1	0
Billy	McEwan	1977/78 - 1978/79	6	0	0	0
Luke	McGee	2016/17	4	0	0	0
John	McGlashan	1993/94	1	0	0	0
Scott	McGleish	1995/96	0	1	1	0
Brian	McGorry	1994/95	2	0	0	0
Johnny	McGuinn	1948/49	2	0	0	1
Leon	McKenzie	2000/01 - 2003/04	7	1	0	1
James	McKeown	2007/08 - 2009/10	0	0	8	0
Aaron	McLean	2006/07 - 2014/15	17	0	0	9
Jamie	McMaster	2004/05	1	0	0	0
Chris	McMenamin	1997/98	2	0	1	0
Peter	McNamee	1958/59 - 1964/65	27	0	0	9
Luke	McShane	2004/05 - 2006/07	1	0	2	0
Dave	McVay	1980/81	6	0	0	0
Nathan	Mendez-Laing	2010/11 - 2014/15	1	5	2	1
Dave	Metchick	1967/68	2	0	0	0
Ricky	Miller	2016/17	0	1	2	0
Tony	Millington	1966/67 - 1968/69	8	0	0	0

First Name	Surname	Period	Apps	Sub	Un-used	Goals
James	Mills	1949/50	1	0	0	0
Adam	Mitchell	1946/47	6	0	0	2
Gavin	Mitchell	1935/36	1	0	0	0
Scott	Mitchell	2007/08	0	1	0	0
Ken	Moody	1951/52 - 1954/55	15	0	0	0
Paul	Moran	1994/95	1	0	0	0
Craig	Morgan	2006/07 - 2009/10	12	1	0	0
Junior	Morias	2017/18	0	2	0	0
David	Morrison	1994/95 - 1996/97	5	3	0	0
Bobby	Moss	1969/70 - 1972/73	5	2	2	2
Ernie	Moss	1976/77	2	0	0	1
Tony	Moulden	1963/64 - 1964/65	3	0	0	0
George	Moulson	1949/50 - 1951/52	8	0	0	0
Bert	Murray	1973/74 - 1975/76	17	0	0	2
Dan	Murray	2000/01 - 2001/02	0	0	2	0
Adil	Nabi	2016/17	0	0	2	0
Jason	Naismith	2018/19	2	1	1	0
Ashley	Neal	1997/98	0	1	0	0
Joe	Neenan	1987/88	2	0	0	0
Joe	Newell	2011/12 - 2014/15	5	2	0	0
Adam	Newton	2002/03 - 2007/08	13	2	1	1
Tom	Nichols	2016/17	3	1	0	1
Mark	Nightingale	1986/87 - 1987/88	3	0	0	0
Jon	Nixon	1974/75 - 1976/77	12	3	0	6
Frank	Noble	1967/68 - 1970/71	10	0	0	0
Matthew	Nolan	2004/05	0	0	1	0
Ritchie	Norman	1968/69	0	0	1	0
Kgosi	Nthle	2013/14 - 2015/16	4	0	2	0
Mick	Nuttell	1986/87 - 1987/88	0	2	0	0
Dennis	Oakes	1971/72 - 1972/73	8	0	0	0
Keith	Oakes	1973/74 - 1990/91	12	1	5	0
Jon	Obika	2010/11	0	1	0	0
Martin	O'Connor	1996/97	2	0	0	0
Nathan	Oduwa	2016/17	0	1	1	0
Nathan	Ofori-Twumasi	2010/11	1	0	1	0
Mark	O'Hara	2018/19	3	1	0	0
David	Oldfield	2000/01 - 2001/02	8	2	1	1
Bobby	Olejnik	2012/13 - 2013/14	5	0	0	0
Conor	O'Malley	2017/18 - 2018/19	4	0	6	0
Lloyd	Opara	2006/07	0	1	1	0
Harry	Orr	1964/65 - 1966/67	10	0	0	1

First Name	Surname	Period	Apps	Sub	Un-used	Goals
Steve	Osbourne	1989/90 - 1990/91	1	2	1	0
Erhun	Oztumer	2014/15 - 2015/16	5	2	0	0
John	Padgett	1946/47	9	0	0	2
Alan	Paris	1985/86 - 1987/88	10	0	0	0
Andy	Parkinson	1979/80	1	0	0	0
Cyril	Parrott	1946/47 - 1950/51	20	0	0	0
Derek	Payne	1996/97 - 1997/98	9	0	0	0
Jack	Payne	2013/14 - 2014/15	5	0	0	0
John	Payne	1969/70	1	0	0	0
Dennis	Pearce	2001/02 - 2002/03	1	0	1	0
Reg	Pearce	1963/64	1	0	0	0
Alex	Penny	2017/18	2	0	3	0
Ian	Phillips	1980/81 - 1981/82	7	0	0	0
Steve	Phillips	1986/87 - 1987/88	2	0	1	0
Tony	Philliskirk	1992/93 - 1993/94	4	0	0	1
Lee	Philpott	1988/89	0	1	1	0
Carl	Piergianni	2010/11	0	0	2	0
Martin	Pike	1983/84 - 1985/86	10	0	0	0
Clive	Platt	2004/05	1	0	0	0
David	Pleat	1970/71	1	0	0	0
Chris	Plummer	2004/05 - 2005/06	2	2	1	0
Jack	Polhill	1945/46	2	0	0	1
Brian	Potts	1969/70	3	0	0	0
Lee	Power	1995/96	1	2	0	0
David	Price	1974/75	2	0	0	0
Paul	Price	1987/88	2	0	0	0
Peter	Price	1969/70 - 1971/72	8	0	0	7
Jon	Pullen	2003/04	0	0	1	0
Gordon	Pulley	1965/66	1	0	0	0
Jimmy	Quinn	1997/98	3	0	0	3
Trevor	Quow	1980/81 - 1985/86	10	1	0	2
Nathan	Ralph	2010/11	0	0	1	0
Frank	Rankmore	1963/64 - 1967/68	17	0	0	0
Jack	Ranshaw	1947/48	4	0	0	2
Colin	Rawson	1947/48	4	0	0	1
Jim	Rayner	1958/59 - 1962/63	24	0	0	5
Simon	Rea	2000/01 - 2003/04	11	0	2	0
Louis	Reed	2018/19	2	1	1	0
Billy	Rees	1958/59	1	0	0	0
Graham	Retallick	1992/93	0	0	1	0
Carl	Richards	1989/90	2	1	0	0

First Name	Surname	Period	Apps	Sub	Un-used	Goals
Justin	Richards	2006/07	0	0	1	0
Michael	Richens	2012/13	0	0	1	0
Tommy	Rickards	1946/47 - 1948/49	16	0	0	6
Graham	Ricketts	1968/69	1	0	0	0
Billy	Rigby	1936/37	4	0	0	0
Norman	Rigby	1951/52 - 1960/61	41	0	0	3
David	Riley	1990/91 - 1991/92	8	0	0	3
Greg	Rioch	1995/96	2	1	0	0
Keith	Ripley	1960/61 - 1961/62	11	0	0	2
Harry	Roberts	1936/37 - 1937/38	6	0	0	2
Lammie	Robertson	1978/79	1	0	0	0
Arnold	Robinson	1949/50 - 1950/51	6	0	0	3
Dave	Robinson	1989/90 - 1991/92	6	0	0	1
Ronnie	Robinson	1992/93	3	0	0	0
Tommy	Robson	1969/70 - 1980/81	43	2	1	10
Billy	Rodaway	1981/82 - 1982/83	6	0	0	0
	Rodgers	1945/46	2	0	0	1
Brian	Ronson	1962/63	3	0	0	0
Ian	Ross	1977/78 - 1978/79	6	0	0	0
Tommy	Ross	1966/67	1	0	0	0
Sam	Rowbotham	1936/37 - 1938/39	12	0	0	1
Tommy	Rowe	2009/10 - 2013/14	5	1	0	1
Zeke	Rowe	1996/97 - 1998/99	4	2	2	0
Tommy	Rudkin	1946/47	8	0	0	6
Allan	Russell	1972/73	1	0	2	0
James	Sage	2012/13	0	0	1	0
Martin	Samuelsen	2015/16 - 2016/17	2	2	0	1
Joe	Sanderson	1948/49	2	0	0	2
Ricardo	Santos	2014/15 - 2016/17	6	0	3	0
Gary	Sargent	1977/78 - 1978/79	4	1	1	2
Thomas	Savage	1937/38	2	0	0	0
Alan	Scobie	1946/47	8	0	0	3
Richard	Scott	1998/99 - 2003/14	1	1	0	0
David	Seaman	1982/83 - 1983/84	5	0	0	0
Ben	Sedgemore	1995/96	1	0	0	0
Ryan	Semple	2003/04 - 2005/06	2	3	2	0
Roy	Senior	1961/62 - 1963/64	7	0	0	1
Pat	Sharkey	1979/80	1	0	0	0
Arthur	Sharp	1938/39	6	0	0	0
Bernard	Shaw	1955/56 - 1958/59	17	0	0	1
Peter	Shearer	1997/98	0	0	1	0

First Name	Surname	Period	Apps	Sub	Un-used	Goals
Jimmy	Sheavills	1962/63	3	0	0	0
Jon	Sheffield	1995/96 - 1996/87	6	0	0	0
Laurie	Sheffield	1970/71	0	0	1	0
Liam	Shephard	2017/18	2	0	1	0
Greig	Shepherd	1985/86	5	1	0	3
Tony	Shields	1999/2000 - 2002/03	4	3	3	1
Kevin	Shoemake	1986/87	1	0	0	0
Len	Silcocks	1946/47	9	0	0	0
Terry	Simpson	1962/63	3	0	0	0
Nigel	Sims	1964/65	3	0	0	0
Syd	Sims	1936/37 - 1938/39	6	0	0	0
Emile	Sinclair	2011/12	1	0	0	0
Tommy	Singleton	1962/63 - 1963/64	4	0	0	0
Graham	Sissons	1962/63 - 1964/65	4	0	0	0
Trevor	Slack	1980/81 - 1985/86	20	0	0	1
Paddy	Sloan	1952/53 - 1953/54	12	0	0	3
Alan	Slough	1977/78 - 1980/81	11	0	0	2
Harold	Smith	1937/38 - 1938/39	8	0	0	0
Jack	Smith	1938/39	5	0	0	0
James	Smith	1937/38	3	0	0	0
Jimmy	Smith	1946/47	5	0	0	0
Keith	Smith	1963/64	2	0	0	0
Michael	Smith	2014/15 - 2016/17	8	1	1	0
Ray	Smith	1956/57 - 1961/62	27	0	0	7
Ray	Smith	1972/73	0	2	0	0
T	Smith	1946/47	3	0	0	0
Tony	Smith	1979/80 - 1981/82	4	0	0	0
Danny	Sonner	2004/05	0	0	2	0
Tony	Spearing	1993/94 - 1996/97	3	3	0	0
Frank	Squires	1947/48	2	0	0	2
Sean	St Ledger	2004/05 - 2005/06	6	0	0	0
Ellis	Stafford	1954/55 - 1959/60	14	0	0	0
Eric	Steele	1974/75 - 1975/76	13	0	0	0
Worrell	Sterling	1989/90 - 1992/93	14	0	0	5
Jude	Stirling	2006/07	2	0	1	0
Gavin	Strachan	2006/07	2	0	0	0
Archie	Styles	1978/79	1	0	0	0
Danny	Swanson	2012/13 - 2013/14	2	2	1	0
Tom	Swinscoe	1951/52	2	0	0	0
Dave	Syrett	1979/80 - 1981/82	4	1	2	1
Ryan	Tafazolli	2016/17 - 2018/19	14	0	0	2

First Name	Surname	Period	Apps	Sub	Un-used	Goals
Doug	Taft	1953/54	4	0	0	3
Fred	Tapping	1948/49	2	0	0	0
Hubert	Tasker	1945/46	1	0	0	1
Jon	Taylor	2014/15 - 2015/16	4	1	0	2
Paul	Taylor	2011/12 - 2016/17	3	2	0	1
Steven	Taylor	2017/18	6	0	0	0
Glen	Thomas	1994/95	0	1	1	0
Josh	Thompson	2011/12	0	0	1	0
Peter	Thompson	1967/68 - 1968/69	3	0	1	1
Steve	Thomson	2003/04 - 2004/05	5	0	2	1
Lee	Thorpe	2005/06	1	0	0	0
Harry	Toffolo	2015/16	0	0	1	0
Lee	Tomlin	2010/11 - 2013/14	7	0	0	3
Ciaran	Toner	2001/02	1	0	0	0
Ivan	Toney	2018/19	3	1	0	4
Sergio	Torres	2008/09	1	1	3	0
Ryan	Tunnicliffe	2011/12	1	0	0	0
Ben	Turner	2006/07	0	0	1	0
Chris	Turner	1969/70 - 1977/78	33	0	1	3
John	Turner	1984/85 - 1985/86	6	0	0	0
Bob	Turpie	1970/71	1	0	0	0
Dick	Tydeman	1983/84	1	0	0	0
Mark	Tyler	1993/94 - 2016/17	33	0	8	0
William	Upton	1935/36	1	0	0	0
Kyle	Vassell	2014/15	1	1	0	0
Glyn	Vaughan	1948/49	4	0	0	1
Ted	Vaux	1949/50	2	0	0	0
Alan	Waddle	1983/84	1	0	0	0
Jamie	Walker	2018/19	0	1	1	0
Jim	Walker	1958/59 - 1962/63	24	0	0	0
Jim	Walker	1975/76	2	0	0	0
Paul	Walker	1973/74 - 1974/75	8	1	1	0
Vic	Walker	1950/51 - 1951/52	5	0	0	0
Jack	Walls	1956/57 - 1961/62	26	0	0	0
Alec	Wands	1949/50	2	0	0	0
Joe	Ward	2018/19	4	0	0	1
	Warner	1945/46	2	0	0	0
Fred	Warnes	1938/39 - 1947/48	17	0	0	5
Ernie	Warren	1935/36	1	0	0	0
Conor	Washington	2014/15 - 2015/16	5	0	0	4
Dale	Watkins	1990/91	1	0	1	0

First Name	Surname	Period	Apps	Sub	Un-used	Goals
Tommy	Watson	1965/66 - 1966/67	5	0	0	6
Keith	Waugh	1976/77 - 1980/81	10	0	0	0
Lewis	Webb	2008/09	0	0	3	0
Steve	Welsh	1991/92 - 1993/94	8	0	0	0
James	Wesolowski	2010/11	2	1	1	0
Chris	Westwood	2007/08 - 2008/09	2	1	3	0
Chris	Whelpdale	2007/08 - 2010/11	8	1	2	0
Ben	White	2018/19	1	0	0	0
Frank	White	1938/39	1	0	0	0
Dick	Whittaker	1960/61 - 1962/63	12	0	0	0
Matthew	Wicks	1999/2000	1	0	1	0
Ted	Widdowfield	1949/50	3	0	0	4
John	Wile	1968/69 - 1985/86	14	0	0	0
Lee	Williams	1994/95 - 1995/96	5	1	0	1
Tom	Williams	2001/02 - 2004/05	9	1	0	0
Harry	Willis	1935/36	1	0	0	0
Roger	Willis	1996/97	5	1	0	0
Calum	Willock	2003/04 - 2005/06	4	3	0	3
Charlie	Wilson	1936/37	5	0	0	0
Jack	Wilson	1936/37	5	0	0	4
Jim	Wilson	1946/47	1	0	0	0
Lawrie	Wilson	2015/16	2	0	0	0
John	Winters	1982/83	4	0	0	0
Kevin	Wood	1952/53 - 1953/54	10	0	0	0
Terry	Woodgate	1954/55	1	0	0	0
Curtis	Woodhouse	2003/04 - 2004/05	6	0	0	1
Nobby (Cliff)	Woods	1945/46 - 1951/52	11	0	0	0
Alex	Woodyard	2018/19	4	0	0	0
Arnold	Woollard	1952/53	7	0	0	0
Scott	Wootton	2011/12	1	0	0	0
Gary	Worrall	1984/85 - 1985/86	8	0	1	1
Roger	Wosahlo	1968/69	1	0	0	0
Ben	Wright	2009/10	0	0	1	0
Brian	Wright	1966/67 - 1971/72	17	0	0	0
Ernie	Wyles	1949/50	3	0	0	0
Simon	Yeo	2006/07	0	2	0	0
Eric	Young	1972/73	3	0	0	0
Gabriel	Zakuani	2008/09 - 2015/16	12	0	2	0

*11 own-goals scored by opposition

Acknowledgements.

Thanks to:

The Posh Supporters Trust for their sponsorship, which helped get this book published.

The
Posh Supporters Trust

The work done by The Posh Supporters Trust is carried out by a small team of dedicated volunteers who are passionate supporters of Peterborough United Football Club.
They are a not-for-profit organisation of supporters, committed to strengthening the voice of fans at Peterborough United Football Club and they seek to improve the links between the club and the community.

For more information on the Posh Supporters Trust
visit their website at: www.theposhtrust.co.uk
email them at: theposhtrust@yahoo.co.uk

The Posh Supporters Trust is registered as a Society under the Co-operative and Community Benefit Societies Act 2014. Registration No. 29533R with the Financial Conduct Authority

Thanks also to:

Club Historian **Peter Lane**, and Club Legend **Peter McNamee**, for agreeing to write Forewords for this book.
Alan Swann, for all his help and assistance.
Barry Miles, for helping with the design of the front cover.
Finally, thanks to Club Statistician **Mick Robinson**, whose input in producing this book was invaluable.

Information Sources.

The Official History of Peterborough United FC by Mick Robinson and Andy Groom.
Peterborough United: The Modern Era by Matt Hill.
Peterborough United: Who`s Who? by Matt Hill.

www.uptheposh.com (online database)
www.theposhtrust.co.uk (online museum)

Reports based on the original match reports from the Peterborough Standard, Peterborough Telegraph, The Citizen and Advertiser and other local newspapers of the time.

SD - #0016 - 070726 - C0 - 210/148/8 - PB - 9781784566685 - Gloss Lamination